Rosicrucian Trilogy

Rosicrucian Trilogy

Fama Fraternitatis, 1614

Confessio Fraternitatis, 1615

The Chemical Wedding of Christian Rosenkreuz, 1616

*The Three Original Rosicrucian Publications
in new translations by*

Joscelyn Godwin, Christopher McIntosh,
& Donate Pahnke McIntosh

WEISER BOOKS

First published in 2016 by Weiser Books
with offices at:
65 Parker Street, Suite 7
Newburyport, MA 01950
www.redwheelweiser.com

© 2016 by Joscelyn Godwin, Christopher McIntosh,
& Donate Pahnke McIntosh

All rights reserved. No part of this publication may be reproduced or transmitted in any form or by any means, electronic or mechanical, including photocopying, recording, or by any information storage and retrieval system, without permission in writing from Red Wheel/Weiser, LLC. Reviewers may quote brief passages.

ISBN: 978-1-57863-603-7 (paperback)
ISBN: 978-1-57863-609-9 (hardcover)

Library of Congress Control Number: 2016947886

Design by Kathryn Sky-Peck

The cover art is a colorized version of Emblem 30, from Michael Maier's *Atalanta Fugiens*, 1617. The line drawings in *The Chemical Wedding of Christian Rosenkreuz* are by Hans Wildermann, first published in *Chymische Hochzeit Christiani Rosenkreutz anno Domini MCCCCLIX. Verfasst von Joh. Val. Andreae. Mit achtundzwanzig Federzeichnungen von Hans Wildermann* (Regensburg: Gustav Bosse Verlag, 1923). Vol. 5 in the series "Regensburger Liebhaberdrucke."
Printed in the United States of America
EB
10 9 8 7 6 5 4 3 2 1

Table of Contents

Preface vii

I. *Fama Fraternitatis* I
   translated by Christopher McIntosh and Donate Pahnke McIntosh,
   and introduced by Christopher McIntosh

   Introduction, 3
   Text, 15

II. *Confessio Fraternitatis* 33
    translated and introduced by Joscelyn Godwin

    Introduction, 35
    Text, 41

III. *The Chemical Wedding of Christian Rosenkreuz* 53
     translated and introduced by Joscelyn Godwin

     Introduction, 55
     Text, 61

About the Translators 184

Preface

Four hundred years ago, the publication of three anonymous documents launched the Rosicrucian movement: the *Fama Fraternitatis* (1614), the *Confessio Fraternitatis* (1615), and the *Chemical Wedding of Christian Rosenkreuz* (1616). Much has been written and argued about the Rosicrucian movement—be it myth, hoax, or spiritual phenomenon (depending on who is speaking about it)—and interest in it is far from extinct. The story of Christian Rosenkreuz and his secretive order, as told in the *Fama Fraternitatis*, had political repercussions that continue to this day, while the *Chemical Wedding* is a landmark in European fantasy fiction.

The present book serves a purpose that should have been served long ago. It is simply to offer those three founding documents in reliable, readable, modern English, while still maintaining the unique voice of their original author. The last time they were translated directly into English was in the 17th century, an era whose language, for all its eloquence, puts up barriers that today's readers should be spared. The accompanying editorial material is intended simply to introduce and explain the historical context, not to interpret the Rosicrucian writings. Our hope is to thereby bring this fascinating material to a wider readership.

I.
FAMA FRATERNITATIS

*Manifesto of the Most Praiseworthy
Order of the Rosy Cross,
addressed to all the rulers, estates, and
learned of Europe*

Translated from the original German and annotated by
Christopher McIntosh *and* Donate Pahnke McIntosh,
with an introduction by Christopher McIntosh

Allgemeine vnd General
REFORMATION,
der gantzen weiten Welt.

Beneben der
FAMA FRA-
TERNITATIS,
Deß Löblichen Ordens des
Rosenkreutzes / an alle Gelehrte
vnd Häupter Europæ geschrieben:

Auch einer kurtzen RESPONSION, von dem Herrn Haselmeyer gestellet / welcher deßwegen von den Jesuitern ist gefänglich eingezogen / vnd auff eine Galleren geschmiedet:

Itzo öffentlich in Druck verfertiget / vnd allen trewen Hertzen communiciret worden.

Gedruckt zu Cassel / durch Wilhelm Wessell /

ANNO M. DC. XIV.

Title page of the first edition of the Fama (Kassel, 1614)

Introduction to the *Fama*

The *Fama Fraternitatis*, first published in Kassel in 1614, is the first of the three so-called Rosicrucian manifestos, the two others being the *Confessio Fraternitatis* (1615) and the *Chymische Hochzeit Christiani Rosenkreutz (Chemical Wedding of Christian Rosenkreuz)* (1616). In order to appreciate fully the impact of the original publication on its readers, we need to understand something of the cultural and religious context in which it appeared. The period in question was approximately a century after the Reformation. Europe was split into opposing religious camps—Protestant and Catholic—and the tensions between them were soon to erupt into the Thirty Years War. In this unsettled atmosphere there were many who sought consolation in millennialism and the expectation of an imminent new age. Here we have one of the key elements of the worldview that underpins the *Fama*.

While generally rejected by the mainstream of the Church, millenarian ideas were a persistent heterodox current in Christendom, transmitted by various prophetic visionaries, who often attracted considerable followings. One of these visionaries stands out as being of seminal importance, namely Joachim of Fiore (1135–1202), a 12th-century Calabrian abbot and mystic.[1] Joachim saw history as proceeding in three successive ages, each presided over by one of the three persons of the Trinity. First came the Age of the Father, characterized by the ethos of the Old Testament and the rule of the Law. Second came the Age of the Son, with the emphasis on the Gospels and on faith. Finally there would come the Age of the Holy Spirit or Paraclete, an age of love, joy, and freedom,

---

1 See Marjorie Reeves' *Joachim of Fiore and the Prophetic Future* (London: SPCK, 1976).

when knowledge of God would be revealed directly in the hearts of all humankind. Joachim conceived of each age as lasting 42 generations of 30 years each. Since he believed the second age to have begun with the birth of Christ, it followed that the third age would begin in 1260. Meanwhile the way must be paved for the advent of the new age, and this would be achieved by a new order of monks who would preach the Gospel throughout the world. One of these would be a supreme teacher whose task it would be to turn the world away from earthly things and toward the things of the spirit. However, for three and a half centuries before the Third Age finally came there would be a period of purging carried out by the Antichrist, a secular king who would destroy the corrupt and worldly Church to make way for the true Church. The Antichrist, in his turn, would be overthrown and the Age of the Spirit would begin. Joachim's influence was transmitted through widely disseminated manuscripts of his writings, and in the 16th century printed editions began to appear along with the works of other prophetic writers.

Such millenarian ideas attracted many people who felt that the Reformation had not produced the hoped-for spiritual renewal, and that a new and more radical Reformation was necessary. These radical reformers emphasized inner experience, virtuous living, and the feeling and emotional side of religion, as against what they saw as the ossified dogmatism that characterized the mainstream Protestant churches.

The radical Reformation worldview was not confined to religion. Those who looked forward to the new dispensation believed that it was going to involve all aspects of life including science, medicine, and the arts. When they looked around them, they saw signs and portents of this. Recently Galileo had pointed a telescope at the moon for the first time. Copernicus had placed the sun at the center of the planetary system. The Americas had been discovered. The globe had been circumnavigated. Everywhere a great expansion of horizons was taking place, and there was a sense that humankind was facing an opportunity to create a new

Paracelsus (1493–1541)

and better world. This mindset often went hand in hand with the notion of an ancient esoteric wisdom, encompassing such currents of thought as Gnosticism, Neoplatonism, Hermeticism, astrology, alchemy, and the Kabbalah.

Of key importance within the currents that fed into the Rosicrucian movement was the heritage of the 16th-century alchemist and physician Theophrastus Bombastus von Hohenheim (1493–1541), who became known as Paracelsus. The philosophy and worldview of Paracelsus amounted virtually to an alternative religion, which came to be called the Theophrastia Sancta, based on the idea of two "lights," the light of grace and the light of nature. It was profoundly disliked by the traditional clergy of both confessions and by the orthodox medical establishment, but it gained many followers among those who were seeking a new religious dispensation.

A highly important prophetic writer in the pre-Rosicrucian period was the Württemberg scholar Simon Studion (1543–1606), author of a vast manuscript entitled the *Naometria* (the Measurement of the Holy Place), which remained unpublished but attained wide influence. In Studion's vision, Joachim's three ages become four and are linked with the four beings of Ezekiel's vision,[2] which became the symbols of the four gospels, namely the angel, the bull, the eagle and the lion. In one of Studion's symbolic drawings these symbols are combined with a millenarian chronology and the idea of the New Jerusalem, which is shown enclosed by four walls bearing the four symbolic images and inscribed with a series of dates. At the end of the wall bearing the eagle is the date 1620, marking the transition to the wall bearing the lion. So evidently Studion saw 1620 as marking the end of the age of the eagle and the beginning of the age of the lion.

By the early years of the 17th century, the atmosphere of prophetic expectation in central Europe had heated up to an intense degree. And this atmosphere was heightened by certain remarkable astronomical events. In 1602 a "new star" (actually a comet) appeared in the constellation of Cygnus, the Swan. In 1603, Johannes Kepler (1571–1630) observed a close conjunction of Saturn and Jupiter in Pisces, which he believed to be the same configuration as that which occurred at the birth of Christ. Kepler consulted a famous Jewish astronomer and rabbi, Isaac Abrabanel, who excitedly proclaimed that the conjunction signified the birth of great prophets and miracle workers, and perhaps even of the Messiah.[3] A few months later, the planet Mars joined the conjunction, which in 1604 moved into Sagittarius, one of the three "fire" signs (the "fiery trigon"). In October 1604, an even more remarkable event took place when a new star, a supernova, blazed forth in the constellation of Serpens, the Serpent.

---

[2] Ezekiel 1:4-26.
[3] Tobias Churton, *Invisibles: The True History of the Rosicrucians* (Hersham, UK: Lewis Masonic, 2009), pp. 10-11.

Coming close on the heels of the conjunction in the "fiery trigon," this appeared to be more than coincidence. Now Kepler became even more excited, speculating that the supernova might be a new star of Bethlehem. The year is crucial, too, in the Rosicrucian story, for working from Christian Rosenkreuz's birth in 1378, as given in the *Confessio Fraternitatis*, the date of the opening of his tomb can be calculated as 1604.

We also need to look at the political dimension of these prophecies. The expectation of a great leader who would usher in a new age was especially strong on the Protestant side, and there were many people who focused their hopes on the Elector Frederick V of the Palatinate, who was married to Elizabeth, the daughter of James I of England. Frances Yates, in her book *The Rosicrucian Enlightenment*, argues that millenarian prophecies "may have helped to decide the Elector Palatine and the enthusiasts behind him to make that rash decision to accept the Bohemian crown in the belief that the millennium was at hand."[4]

It was against this background that the *Fama Fraternitatis* burst onto the stage of Europe. While its exact origins remain a mystery, the evidence points to its having originated from a circle in Tübingen that included the Protestant theologian Johann Valentin Andreae (1586–1654), the Paracelsian physician Tobias Hess (1558–1614), and the jurist Christoph Besold (1577–1638). Hess is thought to have played a key role in distributing manuscripts of the *Fama*, which were circulating from at least 1610.[5] In that year, one of them came into the hands of the Tyrolean notary and Paracelsian physician Adam Haslmayr (c.1555–1630), who issued the first printed reply to the Brotherhood in 1612.[6] Through his alchemist friend Carl Widemann, Haslmayr passed the manuscript of the *Fama* on to Prince August von Anhalt (1575–1653), who read it with

---
4 Frances A. Yates, *The Rosicrucian Enlightenment* (London: Routledge & Kegan Paul, 1972), p. 35.
5 *Cimelia Rhodostaurotica. Die Rosenkreuzer im Spiegel der zwischen 1610 und 1660 entstandenen Handschriften und Drucke*. Exhibition catalogue, compiled and introduced by Carlos Gilly (Amsterdam: In de Pelikaan, 1995), p. 29.
6 Adam Haslmayr, *Antwort An die lobwürdige Brüderschafft der Theosophen von RosenCreutz* (n.p., 1612).

The first page of one of the four surviving German manuscripts of the Fama (Library of the Wellcome Institute, London, MS 150, Bl. 129r–139r).

The Protestant theologian J. V. Andreae (1586–1654), probably the main author of the Fama

enthusiasm, initiated a search for the Brotherhood, and had Haslmayr's reply published in the hope of drawing them out.[7]

Turning to the content of the *Fama*, essentially the text proclaimed the need for a new and radical Reformation and looked toward a new age in Europe, which would bring together science, religion, and ancient wisdom. This message was cloaked in a story about one Christian Rosenkreuz, a German monk and nobleman, who made a journey through the Middle East, gathering wisdom and knowledge from the sages of that region, and then came back to Germany and founded a secret brotherhood called the "Brotherhood of the Rosy Cross." The *Fama* included an appeal to "all the learned of Europe" to enter into communication with the Brotherhood.

---
7   Gilly, *Cimelia Rhodostaurotica*, p. 32.

While it is doubtful whether Christian Rosenkreuz or his fraternity ever actually existed, the publication of the *Fama* established the legend of the Rosicrucian Brotherhood and captured the imaginations of many. It set off a flood of publications in what has become known as the Rosicrucian furore. Some of these were open requests to join the Rosicrucians, some were anti-Rosicrucian salvos, some were by alleged members of the Brotherhood, and some were by writers who took up the Rosicrucian idea and presented their own version of it. An important figure in the last category was the physician and alchemist Michael Maier (1569–1622), one of the main apologists for Rosicrucianism in Germany and author of several books defending the Brotherhood. Maier visited England and probably met his fellow physician and alchemist Robert Fludd (1574–1637), a prolific English apologist for Rosicrucianism.

From the German lands the *Fama* spread far and wide, stirring up controversy not only in Britain but also in France, Holland, Sweden, and elsewhere. In Britain several manuscripts of the *Fama* circulated, but the first printed edition only appeared in 1652.[8] It was linked with the name of the Welsh mystical writer and alchemist Thomas Vaughan (1621–1666),[9] although in fact he was not the translator, whose identity is unknown (here for convenience we speak of the "Vaughan version"). Until now, this was almost the only readily available English translation of the *Fama*, and one which, though elegant in language, does little justice to the original. The text contains errors which, far from being minor, are serious howlers that butcher the original meaning and in some cases convey exactly the opposite one.

The task of producing a scholarly modern English translation for this current book proved to be full of difficulties. Apart from archaic

---

8 *The Fame and Confession of the Fraternity of the R: C: Commonly, of the Rosie Cross. With a Praeface annexed thereto, and a short Declaration of their Physicall Work.* By Eugenius Philalethes [pseudonym for Thomas Vaughan] (London: Giles Calvert, 1652).
9 See entry on Thomas Vaughan by Alan Redrum in Wouter Hanegraaff et al. (eds.), *Dictionary of Gnosis and Western Esotericism* (Leiden: Brill, 2005), Vol. 2, pp. 1157-59.

> # THE
> # FAME
> ## AND
> # CONFESSION
> ### OF THE
> # FRATERNITY
> ### OF
> # R: C:
> #### Commonly, of the
> # Rosie Cross.
>
> WITH
> A Præface annexed thereto, and a short
> Declaration of their Physicall
> Work.
>
> By EUGENIUS PHILALETHES.
>
> Jarch: apud Philostrat:
> Καὶ γὰρ κέρδος εἴη, μήτε πιστεύῃν,
> μήτε ἀπιστεῖν πᾶσιν.
>
> *Veritas in Profundo.*
>
> *London*, Printed by *J.M.* for *Giles Calvert*, at the black spread Eagle at the West end of Pauls. 1652.

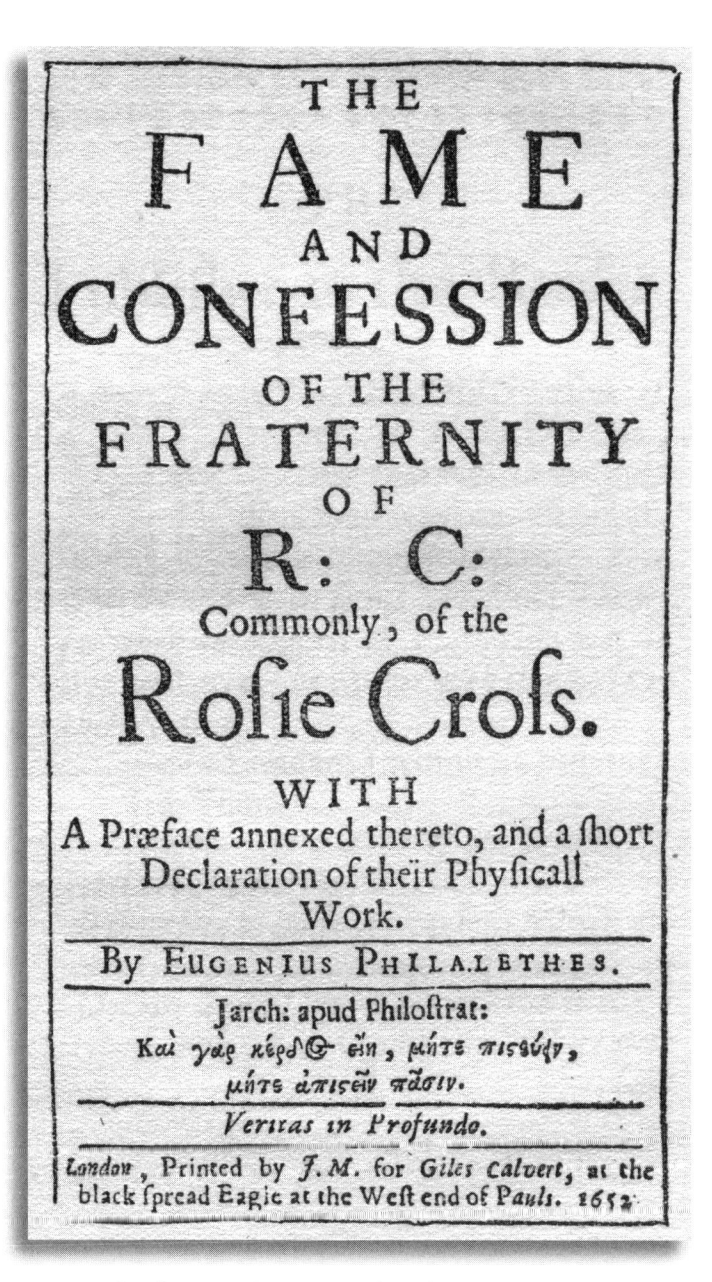

The title page of the 1652 English edition of the Fama

German, inconsistent grammar, and opaque phrases, expressions, and references, there was also the problem of which version of the text to use. There are significant variations from one manuscript to another, between the manuscripts and the printed texts, and between the various printed editions. So, in order to produce an English translation, it was necessary to make careful comparisons between different versions.

Here we have reason to be grateful to others who have brought out scholarly editions of the manifestos. Richard van Dülmen's edition of 1973[10] was a useful starting point, although it relies only on the printed texts and not on the manuscripts. A more in-depth edition is that of Roland Edighoffer (2010),[11] which exhaustively compares the printed text of 1614 with the various manuscripts. In particular we must salute the work of Carlos Gilly in scrutinizing and comparing the original Rosicrucian texts—in both manuscript and printed form—see for example his catalogue for an exhibition of Rosicrucian books and manuscripts held in 1995 at the Ritman Library in Amsterdam.[12] We also need to acknowledge the valuable edition of the *Fama* prepared by Pleun van der Kooij, co-edited and introduced by Gilly, accompanied by a modern German version of the text by Käte Warnke-Specht.[13] Our translation is essentially based on van der Kooij's version. For those readers who are interested in further study of the *Fama*, we have, in a separate

---

10 Andreae, Johann Valentin, *Fama Fraternitatis—Confessio Fraternitatis—Chymische Hochzeit Christiani Rosencreütz. Anno 1459*. Edited and introduced by Richard van Dülmen (Stuttgart: Calwer Verlag, 1973).
11 Andreae, Johann Valentin, *Gesammelte Schriften. Band 3: Rosenkreuzerschriften. Allgemeine Reformation der gantzen weiten Welt (1614)—Fama Fraternitatis R. C. (1614)—Confessio Fraternitatis R. C. (1615)—Chymische Hochzeit Christiani Rosencreütz (1616)*. Edited and with a commentary and introduction by Roland Edighoffer (Stuttgart-Bad Cannstatt: Frommann-Holzboog, 2010).
12 *Cimelia Rhodostaurotica*, see note 6 above. For this and other works by Gilly, see the website of the Ritman Library: http://www.ritmanlibrary.nl
13 Pleun van der Kooij and Carlos Gilly (eds.), *Fama Fraternitatis. Das Urmanifest der Rosenkreuzer Bruderschaft zum ersten Mal nach den Manuskripten bearbeitet, die vor dem Erstdruck von 1614 entstanden sind durch Pleun van der Kooij. Mit einer Einführung über die Entstehung und Überlieferung der Manifeste der Rosenkreuzer von Carlos Gilly* (Haarlem, Netherlands: Rozenkruis Pers, 1998).

publication[14] provided an in-depth, annotated text with added further footnotes, commenting on certain passages, pointing out ambiguities, and drawing attention to some of the main errors in the Vaughan version, together with additional introductory material and scholarly apparatus.

The task of making the English translation was shared by myself and my wife Dr. Donate Pahnke McIntosh, who in addition was solely responsible for a new version in contemporary German, published as a separate volume.

---

14 *Fama Fraternitatis 1614–2014*. Translated from the original German and annotated by Christopher McIntosh and Donate Pahnke McIntosh, with an introduction by Christopher McIntosh (Vanadis Texts, 2014, ISBN 9781499555486).

Fama Fraternitatis

We the Brethren of the Fraternity of the R.C. extend our greetings, love, and prayers to all who read this our *Fama* in a Christian spirit.

God, the all-wise and all-merciful, having in recent times so abundantly poured out his mercy and goodness to humankind that knowledge of his Son and of nature is becoming more and more widespread and we can justly rejoice in a forthcoming happy time, He has not only revealed half of the unknown and hidden world and laid before us many wondrous and hitherto never experienced works and creations of nature, but has also caused certain highly illuminated minds to come forth, who might partially renew the arts, which have become debased and imperfect, so that finally Man might understand his true nobility and splendor, in what sense he is a microcosm, and how far his art extends into nature.

This will of course be of little use to the unthinking world. Laughter, mockery, and malicious talk are on the increase, and even the learned are so full of pride and ambition that they do not wish to come together and, out of everything that God in our age has so richly revealed to us, create a book of nature or a perfect development of all the arts. Rather, every faction among them opposes every other. Furthermore they cling to the old teachings, esteeming the Pope, Aristotle, and Galen—indeed everything that has the appearance of a codex—more than the clear and manifest light. If men such as Aristotle and Galen were alive today they would doubtless be extremely happy to revise their doctrines. But here people are too weak for such a great work. Although in theology, physics, and mathematics truth is working for the opposite, nevertheless the old enemy, with his great cunning and malevolence, is doing his best to discredit and hinder it through the agency of fanatical, discontented, and wayward people.

One who long and avidly strove for such a general reformation was the pious, spiritual and highly illuminated Pater, Fr. C.R., a German, the head and founder of our fraternity.

In the fifth year of his life, because of the poverty of his (nonetheless noble) parents, he was placed in a monastery where he acquired a fair knowledge of both Greek and Latin. While still in the bloom of youth he was, at his own fervent plea, assigned to a certain Brother P. a. L., who had undertaken to make a journey to the Holy Sepulchre.

Although this Brother died in Cyprus and never saw Jerusalem, yet our Brother C.R. did not turn back, but sailed on and journeyed to Damascus, intending to go from there to Jerusalem.

However, sickness detained him in Damascus, where he won favor among the Turks through medicine (in which he was not inexperienced). During his sojourn there he heard by chance about the wise men of Damcar in Arabia and the great wonders they performed and how nature was an open book to them. This inspired his high and noble mind to such an extent that Jerusalem was no longer as high in his thoughts as Damcar. Being unable to restrain his eagerness, he persuaded certain of the Arabian masters in return for a sum of money to convey him to Damcar.

He was only sixteen years of age when he arrived there, but of a strong German physique. There the wise received him, as he avers, not as a stranger but as someone whom they had long expected, calling him by his name and mentioning unknown facts about his monastery, causing him great astonishment. There he learned the Arabic language better, so that the following year he was able to translate into good Latin the Book M., which he afterward brought back with him. It was from here that he took his physics and mathematics, which ought to have been joyfully received by the world if only there were more love and less resentment.

After three years he went on his way again, well enlightened, departing by ship from the Arabian peninsula and proceeding to Egypt, where he remained for only a short time, although long enough to gain a better knowledge of its flora and fauna. He then sailed along the whole length of the Mediterranean Sea to Fez, whither he had been directed by the Arabians. It puts us to shame that wise men, so far remote from each other, should not only be of one mind, rejecting all contentious writings, but also be so willing and ready to reveal their secrets to others in trust and openness.

Every year the Arabians and Africans send representatives to meet with each other, to question one another concerning their arts, and to ascertain whether there have been any new and improved inventions or whether their existing systems of knowledge have been weakened by experience. In this way every year something is brought to light for the improvement of mathematics, physics and magic (in which the inhabitants of Fez excel). Since in Germany at this time there is no lack of scholars, magi, Kabbalists, physicians and philosophers, either they should be better disposed to each other or, if the majority do not want that, then each must eat up the whole meadow alone.

At Fez he made the acquaintance of the Elementary Inhabitants (as he commonly called them), who revealed to him much of what they knew, just as we Germans could do among ourselves if we had sufficient unity and a passionate and earnest desire to search.

Of these people of Fez he often said that their magia was not altogether pure and that their Kabbalah was tainted by their religion. Nevertheless he knew how to make good use of the same and thereby found an even better foundation for his own belief, a foundation which is in exact harmony with the whole world, and whose impress is wonderfully evident in all periods of time.

Thence arises the recognition of the beautiful unity whereby, just as every seed contains the whole tree and its fruit, so likewise the whole world is contained in miniature in every human being, with his religion, politics, health, bodily parts, natural traits, speech, words and works—all of which partake of the same tune and melody as God, heaven, and earth. Everything to the contrary would be error, falsehood, and of the Devil, who is the first, middle and last cause of worldly strife, blindness, and darkness. So if one were to examine each and every person on the globe one would find that what is good and true is always at one with itself, while its opposite is marked by a thousand aberrant opinions.

After two years Frater R.C. left Fez and travelled with many precious treasures to Spain, hoping, as he had so profited from his journey, that the learned of Europe would greatly rejoice with him and thenceforth base all their studies on such true foundations. He therefore discoursed with the learned of Spain about the shortcomings of our arts and how they can be remedied, whence to take certain portents of future times and how they agreed with earlier ones. He spoke of how the deficiencies of the Church and of our moral philosophy could be remedied. He showed them new plants, new fruits, and animals that did not accord with the old philosophy, and gave them new axiomata whereby all [difficulties] might be overcome.

But to them it was all a laughing matter. Because these things were new to them they were worried that their great reputation would be diminished if they now began to learn afresh and if they admitted that they had been in error for many years. They were accustomed to their own errors, which had indeed brought them profit enough; so [they said] let someone else who is served with disquietude reform.

The same little song was sung to him by other nations, which moved him all the more as he had not in the least reckoned with it and was now prepared to share generously all his knowledge and skills with the learned, if they would only take the trouble to probe all faculties, sciences and arts, and all of nature in order to determine certain infallible axioms which, as he knew, would be oriented like a globe toward a single centre and, as is the custom among the Arabians, should serve as a guiding rule for the learned alone, so that also in Europe there might be a society possessing enough gold and precious stones to share with kings along with appropriate guidelines, according to which the rulers could be educated, who would thus know everything that God has imparted to humankind and could be consulted in case of need (as reportedly the idols of the heathens were in former times).

We must certainly recognize that the world in those days was already pregnant with great commotion and was laboring to give birth, and that she brought forth tireless, worthy men who forcefully broke through the darkness and barbarism, leaving us weaker ones to press on after them. Assuredly, they were the tip of the fiery triangle, whose flames will now shine more brightly and give the final illumination to the world.

Such a one, in his calling, was Theophrastus, who did not join our Fraternity, but had diligently read the Book M, whereby his sharp mind was ignited. But this man was so hindered, even at the height of his career, by the machinations of the pedants and pseudo-sages that he could never discuss his thoughts about nature with others. Therefore in his writings he was more intent on mocking these know-alls than on fully revealing himself. Nevertheless, *harmonia* of thought is profoundly present in him, and he would have communicated it to the learned, had he found them to be worthy of the higher art rather than of subtle mocking. So he went on living his free and unconcerned life, leaving the world to its own foolish pleasures.

But, not to forget our beloved Father C.R., he, after many wearisome travels and ill-directed new reformations, returned to Germany, which he dearly loved (by reason of the imminent change and the mighty and perilous struggle to come). There, although he could have boasted of his art, especially that of the transmutation of metals, he set more store by heaven and its human citizens than by all splendor. Nevertheless, he built a fitting and neat habitation, in which he reflected on his travels and on philosophical matters, writing his reflections down in a memoir. In this house he is said to have spent a considerable time preoccupied with mathematics and to have constructed many fine instruments from all branches of this art. Of these, only a few have remained for us, as we shall hear later on.

After five years, there came into his mind again the desired reformation. Because he despaired of the help and support of others, while he himself was industrious, agile, and indefatigable, he undertook to attempt this work with a few helpers and collaborators. Accordingly, from his first monastery (for which he retained great affection) he asked for three of his brethren, namely Fr. G.V., Fr. I. A., and Fr. I. O., who were in addition better versed in the arts than was common at that time. He bound these three to him to be utterly faithful, industrious, and secretive, and to commit to writing with the utmost diligence all that he should instruct them in, so that posterity, should they be admitted by particular revelation, would not be deceived by a single syllable or letter.

Thus began the Brotherhood of the R. C., initially with four persons only, and by them were the magical language and writing provided with an extensive vocabulary, which we still use to this day to God's praise and glory and do find great wisdom therein. They made also the first part of the Book M.

But because that task had grown too large and they were hindered by the arrival of sick people in unbelievable numbers, and since his new building (called Sancti Spiritus) was now finished, they decided to recruit others into their Society and Brotherhood. To this end were chosen Fr. R.C., his deceased father's brother's son Fr. B., a skilful painter, and G.G. and P.D., their scribes, all Germans except for I.A., so in all they were eight in number, all of unmarried state and of avowed virginity. These collected together a large quantity of everything that the human being could wish, desire, or hope for.

Although we freely admit that the world has greatly improved within the past hundred years, yet we are assured that our *Axiomata* will remain unaltered until Judgement Day, and that the world shall see nothing [better] even in its most advanced and ultimate age. For our *Rotae* began on the day that God spoke "*Fiat*" and will remain when God speaks "*Pereat*," yet God's clock strikes every minute, whereas ours hardly strikes the hour.

We also steadfastly believe that, if our fathers and brothers had attained our present bright light they would have more effectively rebuked the Pope, Mahomet, the learned pedants, the philosophers, the artists and the sophists, and would have shown their altruistic disposition not merely with sighs and wishes for fulfilment.

Now when these eight brethren had arranged and taken care of everything in such a way that no further work was necessary and they all had a full grasp of both secret and revealed philosophy, they did not wish to remain any longer together, but, as had been originally agreed, they dispersed to various lands so that not only might their axiomata be more precisely examined in secret by the learned but that they themselves could report to each other whenever, in some country or other, their observations revealed some error. Their agreement was this:

1. None of them should practice any other profession than to cure the sick and that gratis.

2. None should feel constrained on account of the Brotherhood to wear a particular garb, but should wear the attire of the country.

3. Every brother should appear on day C. at the House of the Holy Spirit or state the cause of his absence.

4. Every brother should look about for a worthy person who might succeed him.

5. The word C.R. should be their seal, password, and sign.

6. The Brotherhood should remain undisclosed for one hundred years.

These six articles they vowed to one another to keep, and five of the brethren departed. Only Brothers B. and D. remained with Father C. for a year. When they also departed there remained with him his cousin and Brother I.O., so that for all the days of his life he always had two brethren with him.

And, although the Church was not yet cleansed, we do know what they thought of her and what they awaited with longing desire. Every year they assembled with joy and gave a full account of what they had done. And then it must certainly have been a joyful experience to hear, truly and without invention, of all the wonders that God has now and then strewn throughout the wide world without even having seen it [themselves]. And everyone may hold it for certain that such persons—having been brought together by God and the whole heavenly dispensation and selected by the wisest man in many centuries—lived in the utmost unity, the most scrupulous discretion, and the greatest loving kindness among themselves and among others.

In such a praiseworthy manner did they conduct their lives, and, although their bodies were freed from all diseases and pains, yet their souls could not go beyond [delay] the appointed moment of release.

The first of this Fraternity who died, and that in England, was I.O., as Fr. C. had long before predicted to him. He was very skilled and learned in the Kabbalah, as witness his book H. In England he is much spoken of, especially because he cured a young earl of Norfolk of leprosy.

They had decided that, as far as possible, their burial places should remain hidden, so that today the whereabouts of various of these are unknown to us. Yet in place of each one of them a capable successor was appointed.

Here we wish, to the honor of God, publicly to make known that, whatever secrets we may have learned from the *Book of Mysteries* (how we can have before our eyes the image and counter-image of the whole world), neither our misfortunes nor the hour of our death are known to us, as the great God reserves these to himself, wishing to have us in readiness.

But more of this in detail in our *Confessio*, in which we set out thirty-seven reasons why we now reveal our Brotherhood and offer such high mysteries freely and without compulsion or any reward. Also we promise more gold than the King of Spain brings from the Indies, for Europe is with child and will bring forth a strong child, who shall stand in need of a great godfather's gift.

After the death of O. Fr. C. did not rest but, as soon as he could, called the others together. It seems that it was only then that his grave was made.

Although we (the more recent ones) up to now did not know when our dear Father Fr. R.C. died and had no more than the mere names of the founders and all their successors up to ourselves, yet we remembered a secret which was entrusted to us of the third generation by A., the successor of D. (who was the last of the second succession of brethren and who had lived with many of us), when he spoke cryptically of a period of one hundred years.

Furthermore we must confess that, after the death of A., none of us had the least knowledge of R.C. and his initial fellow brethren, apart from what was left of them in our Philosophical Library, among which our *Axiomata* was considered by us to be the work of the highest rank, *Rotae Mundi* the most elaborate, and *Proteus* the most useful. Therefore we do not know for certain whether those of the second succession possessed wisdom equal to those of the first and whether they had been given access to everything.

We shall, however, shortly remind the gracious reader that what we not only know about the burial of Fr. C., but hereby publicly declare, was ordained, permitted and enjoined to us by God. This we fulfil with such faithfulness that, if anyone shall give us a modest and Christian reply, we shall not hold back from revealing in open print our Christian and surnames, our meetings, and whatever else may be desired.

Here then is the true and thorough account of the discovery of the highly illuminated man of God, Fr. C.R.C.

After A. had beatifically passed away in Gallia Narbonensis,[1] his place was taken by our beloved Brother N.N. When he found us and

---

[1] That is, the southern French region of Provence.

took the solemn oath of fidelity and secrecy, he confided to us that A. had comforted him by saying that this Fraternity would soon not be so secret, but would be to the whole Fatherland of the German Nation helpful, necessary, and renowned. Of this he had not the slightest reason to be ashamed among his peers.

The following year, having already completed his studies and having the opportunity to travel, equipped with a generous supply of travel money of Fortunatus's purse, he thought (being also a master builder) to make some alterations to this building and arrange it more suitably. In this course of this work he came upon a memorial plaque of brass, bearing the names of all the Brotherhood as well as a few things. This he wished to transfer to another and more suitable vault, for where or when Fr. C. had died, or in what country he might be buried, was by our elders concealed and was unknown to us.

In this plaque was fixed a great nail, so strongly that, when it was forcibly pulled out, it took with it a fairly large piece of masonry from the thin wall or layer covering the hidden door that was thereby unexpectedly revealed. Thereupon we joyfully and eagerly removed the rest of the masonry and cleared the door, on the upper part of which was written [in Latin] in capital letters: AFTER 120 YEARS I SHALL OPEN with the original year underneath.

For this we gave thanks to God and let everything rest for the evening, as we wanted to consult our *Rota*.

Here for the third time we refer to our *Confessio*, for what we reveal here is for the benefit of those who are worthy. To the unworthy, God willing, it will be of little use. For just as our door opened miraculously after so many years, so also shall a door open to Europe (when the masonry is completely removed), which is already beginning to show itself. This is with great eagerness expected by many.

In the morning we opened the door and found a vault of seven sides and corners, each side being five feet wide and eight feet high.

Although the sun never shone in this vault, nevertheless it was brightly lit by another, which had learned from the sun and stood uppermost in the center of the ceiling. In the middle, instead of a gravestone, there was a small round altar, covered with a small plate of brass on which was written [in Latin]:

> *A.C.R.C. This compendium of the universe I made during my lifetime as a tomb for myself.*

Around the first edge or rim stood the words: *Jesus all things to me.* In the middle were four figures, enclosed in a circle, with the following [Latin] circumscription:

1. *A void exists nowhere.*
2. *The yoke of the law.*
3. *The Liberty of the Gospel.*
4. *God's glory is inviolable.*

This was all clear and distinct [to see], as were the seven sides and the twice seven triangles. Therefore we knelt down together and thanked the sole wise, sole mighty, and sole eternal God, who has taught us more than all human reason could find out, praised be His name.

We distinguished three parts of this vault: the ceiling or heaven, the walls or sides, and the ground paving. Of the ceiling you will not hear anything more from us at present, save that it was divided into triangles, running from the bright center toward the seven sides. But what was inside should rather be seen by your own eyes (you who would await salvation) than be received through our description.

Each of these sides was divided into ten quadrilateral sections, containing various figures and sentences, as carefully and accurately described in our attached booklet *Concentratum*.

The floor was also divided into triangles, but, because therein are described the rulership and power of the base regent, it is not exposed to misuse by the frivolous and godless world. However, those who are provided with the heavenly antidote can without fear or hurt tread on the head of the old evil serpent, something for which our age is well suited.

Each side had a door to a chest containing various things, especially all our books, which we already possessed, including the *Vocabulary* of Theophrastus Bombastus of Hohenheim and those that we use daily and of which we faithfully report to others. Herein we also found his itinerary and *vita*, from which most of this work is taken.

In a further chest were mirrors of various good properties, and in other places were little bells, lighted hanging lamps and especially certain marvelously artistic songs. Altogether, everything was arranged in such a way that, were the whole Order or Brotherhood to perish, it would be possible, even after many centuries, to reconstitute it from this unique vault.

We had not yet found the body of our so careful and wise father, so we moved the altar aside, enabling us to lift up a thick plate of brass, revealing a fair and illustrious body, undamaged and completely undecayed, as can be seen most accurately in the picture with all regalia and burial objects.

In his hand he held a book, written in gold on parchment, called T., which, after the Bible, is now our greatest treasure and should not lightly be exposed to the censure of the world. At the end of the book was the following [Latin] eulogy:

> *A grain, buried in the heart of Jesus, Christian Rosenkreuz sprang from the noble and illustrious German family of Rosenkreuz. He was a beacon of his age and an ornament for future centuries. Through divine revelation, highly subtle investigations and tireless efforts he was admitted into the mysteries and secrets of heaven and earth. In his journeys through Arabia and Africa he collected a treasure surpassing that of kings and emperors. However, as it was*

not congenial to his age, he preserved it in an ingenious manner for posterity to uncover. Further, he appointed trusted people and close friends to be the heirs of his arts and also of his name, and he created a miniature world, corresponding in all motions to the greater one. Finally, after he had created this compendium of things past, present and future, being more than a hundred years old, he gave his illuminated soul, not through sickness (which he had never felt in his own body and never allowed others to be afflicted by), but rather summoned by the divine spirit, back to God the creator amid the last kisses of his Brethren. Our much loved Father, most sweet Brother, most faithful teacher and most unblemished friend, he was hidden here by his own kind for 120 years.

Underneath they had signed [in Latin]:

1. Brother I.A, chosen by Brother C. as head of the Fraternity.
2. Brother S.G.V.M.P.S.
3. Brother R.C. junior, inheritor of [the House] of the Holy Spirit.
4. Brother B.M.P.A., painter and master builder.
5. Brother G.G.M.P.I., Kabbalist.

In the second circle [in Latin]:

1. Brother P.A., successor to Fr. I.O., mathematician.
2. Brother A., successor to P.D.
3. Brother R., successor to Father C.R.C. who is rejoicing with Christ.

At the end was written [in Latin]:
WE ARE BORN IN GOD,
WE DIE IN JESUS,
WE LIVE AGAIN IN THE SPIRIT.

Father O. and Father D. at that time already being deceased, where is their place of burial to be found? But we have no doubt that none of the old Brothers would have been buried or perhaps also concealed without something special. We also hope that our example will stir up others to enquire after these people (whose names we have therefore revealed) and to search for their place of burial. For, on account of their medicine, most of them are still known and celebrated among very old people. Thus might our *gaza*[2] be increased or at least better elucidated.

Concerning the *minutus mundus*, we found it kept in another little altar, truly more beautiful than could be imagined by even the most understanding person. This we leave undescribed until such time as we receive confidential replies to our true-hearted *Fama*.

Accordingly, we put back the plate, placed the altar back on top of it, re-closed the door and sealed it with our collective seal. Furthermore, following the instruction and command of our *Rota*, we published various booklets, including the book *M. Hoch.*,[3] composed by the greatly loved M.P. instead of various domestic duties.

Finally, as was our custom, we departed from one another and left our treasures in the possession of their natural heirs. So we await the answer, judgement, or decision of the learned or unlearned.

While we well know that it will still be a fairly long time before the advent of the general divine and human reformation longed for by us or hoped for by others, it is not undue that before the sun rises it casts a bright or dark light in the sky. [Likewise] meanwhile some few, who shall make themselves known, shall come together, [increase] our Brotherhood in number and reputation and make a happy beginning with the desired philosophical canon laid down by Pr. C., or they shall, together with us, enjoy our treasures (which are inexhaustible) in humility and love, sweeten the arduous nature of this world, and not wander blindly in God's marvellous works.

---

2 The Latin word *gaza*, stemming from the Persian, means "treasure," "treasure chamber," or "supply or possession." In this context it probably means a treasure of knowledge. It clearly has nothing to do with the city of Gaza in Palestine.
3 Apparently an abbreviation of *Mystische Hochzeit* (Mystical Wedding), i.e. probably referring to the *Chemical Wedding of Christian Rosenkreuz*, the third of the Rosicrucian manifestos.

However, in order that every Christian shall know of what belief and faith we people are, we hereby confess to the recognition of Jesus Christ, as it has in recent times gone forth brightly and clearly, especially in Germany, and is still today being preserved, defended, and propagated in certain particular and known countries (excluding all zealots, heretics, and false prophets).

We also enjoy two sacraments, as instituted with all formulae and ceremonies of the first renewed Church.

In politics we acknowledge the Roman Empire as the Fourth Monarchy and as supreme for us and all Christians.

As well as the fact that we know what great changes are imminent and would dearly like to make these known to other learned people in writing, this is what we have written. Without God, no one will be able to make us outlawed and give us to the unworthy to be robbed. We shall, however, give hidden aid to the good cause, according to whether our gold permits or prevents it. For our gold is not blind like the Fortuna of the Heathens but serves to bring ornament to the Church and honor to the Temple.

Our Philosophia is nothing new but is the same which Adam received after his fall and which Moses and Solomon applied. Thus she should not greatly doubt or refute other opinions, but, as truth is one, is brief and is always consistent with itself and above all fully in accordance with Jesus in all its parts and members, just as he is the image of the Father, so it [truth] is his likeness. Thus it should not be said: "This is true according to philosophy but false according to theology," for everything which Plato, Aristotle, Pythagoras, and others recognized as true, and which was decisive for Enoch, Abraham, Moses, and Solomon and which above all is consistent with that wonderful book the Bible, comes together, forming a sphere or ball in which all the parts are equidistant from the center. This will be spoken of further and in greater detail in a Christian connection.

Concerning the godless and accursed gold-making, this has gotten so out of hand in our time that many greedy gallows-birds practice great knavery with it and lead people to abuse the curiosity and credulity of many. There are also simple people at this time who are of the opinion that the transmutation of metals is the apex and summit of philosophy, who think that is what it's all about, and that he who can make gold in large quantities and nuggets must be especially pleasing to God, so, with thoughtless pleading or heart-rending sour expressions, they hope to persuade the all-knowing God [himself], who knows all hearts.

We hereby publicly declare this to be false. To the true philosophers, gold-making is a trivial matter and a side issue, in comparison with which they have a thousand better skills. And we say with our dear Father C.R.C.: "Gold *pfui!* if it is nothing more than a bit of gold." For he to whom all of nature is open does not rejoice that he can make gold or, as Christ says, that the devils obey him, but that he sees heaven open, the angels of God ascending and descending, and his name written in the book of life.

We also testify that in the name of alchemy many books and pictures have appeared that are an offence to the glory of God. These we shall name in due course and shall give a catalogue of them to pure hearts. And we ask all learned people to beware of such books, for the enemy never ceases to sow his weeds until a stronger one drives it out of him.

According to the intention of our Father C.R.C., we his brethren for the second time request all the learned of Europe who will read our *Fama* (published in five languages) as well as the Latin *Confessio*, to examine their arts most carefully and searchingly, to reflect seriously upon the present age, and then to consider our offer with a thoughtful mind and reveal to us their thoughts in printed form, either after collective deliberation or individually. For, although neither we nor our community are named at the present time, each person's opinion, in whatever language, shall assuredly reach us.

Furthermore, no one who gives his name shall fail to come into conversation with one of us either orally or (if he has some objection thereto) in writing. Verily we say that whoever has earnest and heartfelt intentions toward us and the future work shall benefit in goods, body, and soul. But he whose heart is false or only greedy for gold shall, firstly, not do us any harm, but shall plunge himself into the greatest and deepest ruin.

And our building, even if a hundred thousand people had seen it from close to, shall forever remain untouched, undestroyed, unseen, and completely hidden from the godless world. *Under the shadow of Thy wings, Jehovah.*[4]

—The Brethren of the Fraternity of the R.C.

---

4 Written in Latin in the original: SUB UMBRA ALARUM TUARUM JEHOVA.

II.
CONFESSIO FRATERNITATIS R.C.

(The Confession
of the Rosicrucian Brotherhood)

To the Learned of Europe

*Translated from the Latin edition of 1615,
with an introduction by* Joscelyn Godwin

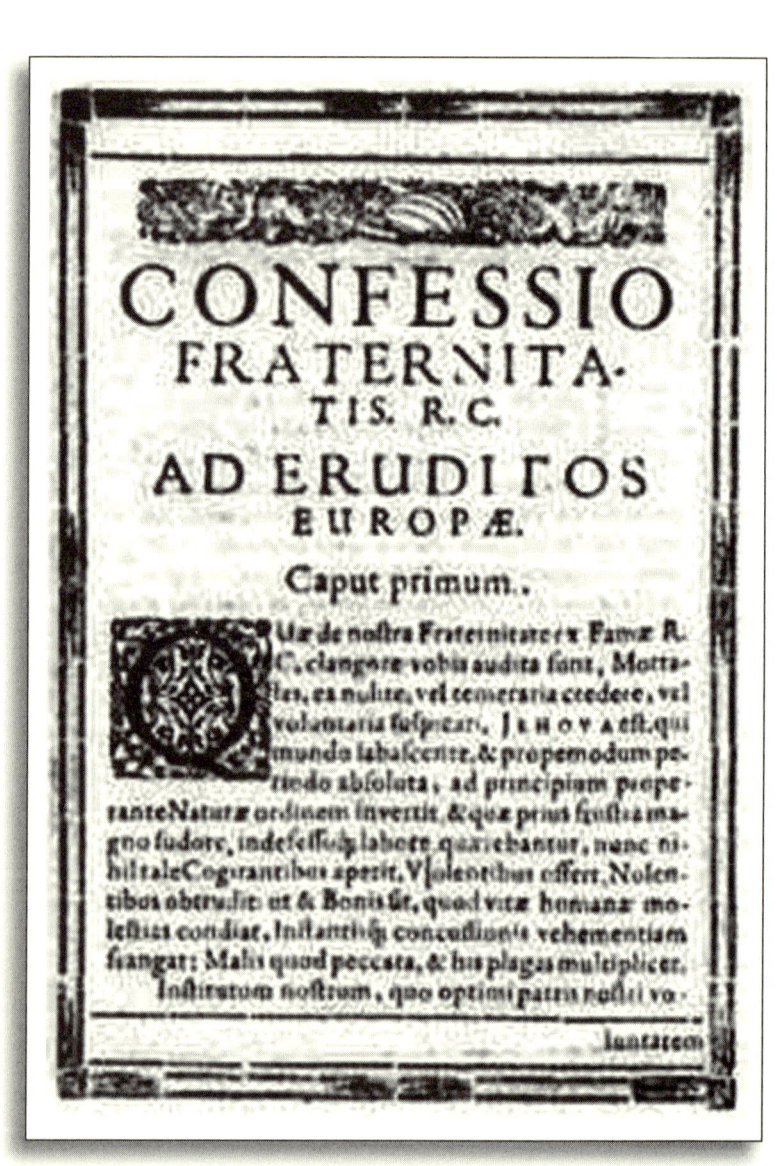

Confessio Fraternitatis

Introduction to the *Confessio*

The *Fama Fraternitatis*, circulating in manuscript since 1610, mentioned "our *Confessio*" and "the Latin *Confessio*" as already existing. Both works were published by Wilhelm Wessel, the court printer of Kassel, with the explicit permission—perhaps even on the orders—of the ruler, Landgraf Moritz of Hessen.[1] Both publications followed the same strategy of prefacing the Rosicrucian manifesto with a longer work. The *Fama* followed an excerpt from a recent satire by Trajano Boccalini (1556–1613),[2] a "fanciful exposure of political, literary, and social absurdities in the form of daily news reports of the occurrences in Apollo's court."[3] The German title trumpeted it as "Universal and General Reformation of the Whole Wide World," giving to the whole publication an aura of exaggeration and even comedy. The *Confessio*, in contrast, was in Latin, tacked on to a difficult alchemical treatise by the otherwise unknown Philippus à Gabella, whose modest title translates as "A Short Consideration of the More Secret Philosophy."[4] It is an alchemical analysis of the "hieroglyphic monad," a figure invented by John Dee (1527–1608/09)[5] and widely circulated at the time. Gabella relates it first to archetypal geometry, then to the solar system, the Arabic numerals, the humors, metals, elements, the macrocosm and

---

1 Gilly, *Cimelia Rhodostaurotica*, pp. 70, 73.
2 Trajano Boccalini, *De' Ragguagli di Parnaso* (Venice: Pietro Farri, 1612).
3 William F. Marquardt, "The First English Translators of Trajano Boccalini's *Ragguagli di Parnaso*: A Study of Literary Relationships," *Huntington Library Quarterly* 15/1 (1951), pp. 1–19. Here quoted: p. 1.
4 *Secretioris philosophiae consideratio brevis, à Philippo à Gabella Philosophiae St[udioso] conscripta, & nunc primùm unà cum Confessione Fraternitatis R. C. in lucem edita* (Kassel: Guilhelmus Wesselius, 1615).
5 John Dee, *Monas hieroglyphica* (Antwerp: Guglielmus Silvius, 1564). The figure appears beside the invitation to the *Chemical Wedding*; see page 64.

the microcosm, the influence of the stars, and the fusion of opposites. Rosicrucian references frame the treatise. It opens with the hope that it might be honored by the study and industry of the "Fraternitas R.C." and ends with the signature "Philemon Philadelphiae R.C."

Scholarly consensus attributes both the *Fama* and the *Confessio* to Johann Valentin Andreae, though with the caveat that his friends, including Tobias Hess and perhaps Christian Besold, had a large part in elaborating the fictive Fraternity. The *Confessio*, which includes many phrases from Hess's work, is a bland document in comparison with the tall tales of the *Fama*, but its purpose is clear: it supplies more learned readers with the doctrinal underpinning of the enterprise. Thus the two manifestos, with their contrasting companion works, are a complementary pair.

Within months of its discreet appearance, the *Confessio* was translated into German. As such, it immediately circulated widely, usually paired with the *Fama* and without the shield of Boccalini's or Gabella's texts. The German *Confessio* became the basis for further translations, including three or more English versions, one in Scottish dialect, and the well-known Vaughan edition of 1652.[6] But none of these is true to the original. The German translator added many flourishes to the succinct and plain spoken Latin, and the English contributed mistakes of their own (some of which were corrected by F. Norman Pryce in his edition of 1923). The extreme rarity of the Latin original, which exists in only a handful of libraries, discouraged investigation. In consequence, every English reissue of the *Confessio* has copied or adapted the Vaughan translation, whose 17th-century diction raises problems that the 21st-century reader

---

6 Two English translations, linguistically related to each other and to Vaughan's edition, are in the Ashmole papers of the Bodleian Library, Oxford: Ms. Ashmole 1478, ff. 127'–129 and Ms. Ashmole 1459, pp. 300–311. Another is in the library of the Royal College of Physicians in Edinburgh: see the transcription in Adam McLean, ed., *A Compendium on the Rosicrucian Vault* (Edinburgh: Hermetic Research Series, 1985), pp. 5–17. On the Scottish manuscript, now in the John Rylands Library, Manchester, see F. Norman Pryce's introduction to a facsimile of Vaughan's *Fame and Confession of the Fraternity of R: C:* (Margate: W.J. Parrett for the Societas Rosicruciana in Anglia, 1923), pp. 3–8.

can well do without. Hence, this new translation. I thank my colleague at Colgate University, Professor John Gallucci, for help with some awkward Latin phrases.

The original *Confessio* is structured in fourteen chapters and contains, so it says, thirty-seven *"rationes"* for the Brotherhood's plan. These are also mentioned in the *Fama*, but where are they? The clue may lie in the Latin text. It is amply punctuated with commas, colons, and semicolons, but after the initial address to the reader, it only comes to a period (full stop) thirty-three times. These, with four question marks, suggest that the "reasons" or "rationales" are the following principles or beliefs:

1. God's current intervention in world history
2. Loyalty to Protestantism and to the Emperor
3. Sickness of current Philosophy
4. A cure for the same arising in Germany
5. The doctrine of the Microcosm as the key to Philosophy
6. Justification for revealing secrets
7. That a new age has begun
8. Supreme value of Rosenkreuz's work
9. Its great advantage to us
10. Resistance to the temptation to keep secrets for ourselves
11. Secrets given not through our merit but by God's grace
12. Secrets not given with preference to rank
13. Nor to those who beg for them
14. Dawn of a new age with new laws, and coming fall of the Papacy

15. Great changes have occurred in the world since Rosenkreuz's time

16. Hint to investigate these

17. God's messages are "inscribed on the world-machine"

18. Immunity of our selves and our treasures till the new Empire comes

19. Coming return of Adamic wisdom

20. Coming abolition of manifold opinions and errors

21. Many thinkers are involved in this beside ourselves

22. God's signs of new stars in the Serpent and the Swan

23. In the coming age, the truth will be not merely sensed, but spoken out loud

24. Studying the alphabet of the heavens can reveal the history of the Church

25. This is our new and best language

26. It is imperative to read the Holy Bible

27. Every letter of the Bible contains clues to understanding the world

28. Studying Nature is better than practicing alchemy

29. Do not waste the advantages of wealth in futile pursuits

30. God exalts the humble and puts down the mighty, especially the Pope

31. Soon the Pope will come to naught

32. Pay no attention to alchemical books

33. Come to us instead, for a simple explanation of the secrets

34. Now you have heard us, what do you think?

35. Will you join us?

36. Nature will reward you

37. But only those who are sincere and chosen by God will find us.

In her book *Rose Cross over the Baltic*, Susanna Åkerman analyzes the Rosicrucian tradition from 1610–1620 into three distinct branches: (1) The deepening of the Protestant reformation, developing through Johan Arndt and Andreae in opposition to the more occult Rosicrucians; (2) The interpretation colored by theosophy and Joachimist millenarianism; (3) The interpretation based on Paracelsism and on planetary, angelic, and talismanic magic.[7] All are latent in the short compass of the *Confessio*, though adherents of the first branch would find fewer "reasons" than the second or third. By the time the manifesto appeared, Andreae had already moved on to a position from which he could dismiss it as part of a *ludibrium*, a jest or prank. Yet he himself would contribute to the most mysterious and occult branch, with the longest and richest of all Rosicrucian documents: the *Chemical Wedding*.

---

7 Summarized from Susanna Åkerman, *Rose Cross over the Baltic: The Spread of Rosicrucianism in Northern Europe* (Leiden: Brill, 1998), p. 95.

Confessio Fraternitatis R.C.

Oear Reader,

You will find here, interspersed with the Confession, thirty-seven reasons for our plan. This allows you to choose and compare them, and to consider whether they are enough for your invitation. It is difficult to be convinced of what is not yet apparent, but when it really comes to light, we think people will be ashamed of such doubts. Indeed, we now openly call the Pope the Antichrist, which used to be a capital crime here! Thus we know that what we used to keep quiet, we shall in future proclaim out loud. Will you, Reader, join in our wish that this may happen with all speed?

—Brotherhood R.C.

The Confession of the Brotherhood R.C., to the learned men of Europe.

CHAPTER ONE

O Mortals, whatever you have heard about our Brotherhood from the uproar around the *Fama*, do not think it casual or wilful on our part! [Reason no. 1] It is JEHOVAH himself, who sees the world tottering almost at the end of its age, and returning to its beginnings. He has reversed the order of Nature, so that what was formerly sought with incessant labor and sweat is now opened up to those who never gave it a thought. He offers it to the violent and forces it on the unwilling. To the good, it eases the troubles of human existence and mitigates the assaults on them; to the wicked, it increases their sins and hence their punishments.

[Reason no. 2] We reckon that our institution, through which we best execute the will of our father, is evident enough from the *Fama*. Nor can we be suspected of any heresies or evil intent toward the Republic. We hate the blasphemies of both East and West (i.e. Mohammed and the Pope) against our Lord Jesus, and offer to the Emperor our prayers, our secrets, and our great store of gold. However, for the sake of the learned we have seen fit to explain more fully what was obscure in the *Fama,* or for certain reasons not published in the other languages. We hope thereby to render them more friendly toward us, and more readily approving of our plan.

CHAPTER TWO

[Reason no. 3] Concerning the repair of Philosophy, so necessary today, we have explained how sickly it is. Indeed, we have no doubt of that, though many pretend that its soul is quite sound.

[Reason no. 4] It often happens that when a new disease arises somewhere, Nature supplies the remedy in that very place. Likewise during these great crises of Philosophy there have arisen means not only suited to our country, but the only ones through which Philosophy can recover, and appear in a new or renewed form for the renovation of the world.

[Reason no. 5] Philosophy for us is nothing less than the chief of all the faculties, sciences, and arts. If we look at our own age, Philosophy embraces much of Theology and Medicine, but little of Law. It carefully anatomizes both heaven and earth; in brief, it sufficiently describes the one man, the Microcosm. If any of the learned are modest enough to appear at our brotherly invitation, they will discover among us far other and greater marvels than they ever believed in, admired, or professed.

CHAPTER THREE

[Reason no. 6] As we explain the essence of our plan, we must be sure of one thing: that while you may marvel at our boldness, it should be clear that we are not profaning the great secrets, nor that it is improper to spread news of them among the multitude. [Reason no. 7] Nor is it surprising that many are overwhelmed by the conflict of opinion at this unhoped-for opportunity of ours. They have not yet come to know the miracles of the Sixth Age, but fear that the revolution of the world will bring a future just like the present. They are so occupied by the distress of the present age that they wander in the world like blind men, who in broad daylight can discern things only by touch.

CHAPTER FOUR

[Reason no. 8] Concerning the first part, we judge that our father Christian's meditations embrace everything invented, refined, and propagated since the world's beginnings out of human ingenuity, divine revelation, the ministry of spirits or angels, the sagacity of mind, or the experience of daily observation. We reckon that if Almighty God should decree the destruction of the entire body of literature, Christian's work alone would serve as the new foundation of the sciences, on which posterity could erect a new citadel of truth. It might well be easier to do so than to repair such a ruined structure, enlarging a courtyard here, letting light into rooms there, and altering the doors, stairs, and other things that represent our intentions. [Reason no. 9] How then could we spurn such things, if they had been given to us alone to know in this way, rather than to the whole age as its ornament? Would we not gladly rest in the one truth, which mortals seek through such circuitous and labyrinthine ways, if God had wanted to light the Sixth Candelabrum[1] for us alone? [Reason no. 10] Would it not be enough for us to fear neither hunger nor poverty, neither sickness nor old age? Would it not be wonderful if you could live at any hour as if at the birth of the world, and as if you would live to the end of it? If you could inhabit a place where neither the inhabitants of the Ganges could hide their deeds from you, nor the Peruvians their councils? If you could read in a single book all the books that ever were, are, and will be; and could understand and remember it

---

1 Allusion to the seven candelabra of Simon Studion's *Naometria*, a scheme of sacred history inspired by Exodus 26:31-37 or Revelation 4:5.

all? If you could sing songs that would to draw to you not rocks but gems, not beasts but spirits; and instead of Pluto, would enchant the most powerful princes of the world's empire?[2] [Reason no. 11] But God's plan, O Mortals, is far otherwise, and so is your advantage, for he has decreed that our Brotherhood should increase and multiply with time. We accept this gladly, since we have been admitted to such treasures through no merit of our own, indeed without hope or expectation. We have acted in the same faith, so that not even pity for our own children (which some of us Brothers have) would sway us. For we know that this unhoped-for benefit is not hereditary, nor given indiscriminately.

CHAPTER FIVE

[Reason no. 12] If someone from the other side should wish us more prudent, thinking that we dispense our treasures too freely and indiscriminately, without favoring the virtuous, the wise, even princes, above the people, we are not angered, for the charge is not invalid. Rather, we confirm that our secrets will not be made public, however much they echo around common ears in five languages. We grant the dignity of Acceptance not according to curiosity, but by the rule and norm of our own revelations. [Reason no. 13] The unworthy may cry out and offer themselves a thousand times: God has charged our ears to hear nothing of them. He has protected us with his clouds, lest anything should hurt his servants, and made us invisible to human eyes, unless they were borrowed from an eagle.

[Reason no. 14] The *Fama* was issued in vernacular languages so as not to cheat those less expert in letters, whom God has not excluded from the joy of this Brotherhood (which is divided by degrees). Likewise the inhabitants of the city of Damar[3] live under a political system far different from the other Arabs, for there the wise predominate, and the king allows them to make other laws. As Father Christian has written, this example will

---

2 Allusion to the myth of Orpheus.
3 A city in the Yemen, miswritten as "Damcar" in the *Fama*.

even be instituted by us in Europe, when what must precede it has taken place. Then our trumpet will sound forth loudly and with no ambiguity of language, and what a few are now murmuring, cloaking the future as far as they can with riddles, will then fill the whole earth. Just so, after worthy men had given the Pope's tyranny many a covert nibble and timid insult, he was cast down from his throne by Germany, with great force and a great crash, and well trampled underfoot. But his annihilation is reserved for our age, when he will be clawed to pieces and the lion's roar will end his braying.[4] We know that it is dawning on many of Germany's learned men, as testified by their signs and silent approbation.

CHAPTER SIX

[Reason no. 15] It would be worthwhile examining that whole period from 1378, when our Christian was born, until today, seeing how much change in the world he witnessed in his 106 years of life, and how much he left after his blessed death to be experienced by our fathers and ourselves. But brevity compels us to leave this to another time. [Reason no. 16] Let that be enough for those who do not spurn our advice, so that they may make preparations for a closer union and friendship with us. [Reason no. 17] Anyone who discerns those great letters that God has inscribed on the world-machine and renewed through all the vicissitudes of empires, and who can understand, read, and inform himself from them, is already one of us, though he may be unaware as yet. We know that he will not ignore our invitation, and for our part we forswear all deceit. We promise that in future no one's sincerity and desire will be laughed at because of us, when he offers himself under the seal of silence and asks for a relationship. [Reason no. 18] As for those frauds and impostors who desire anything but wisdom, they cannot lead us to our ruin, nor force us to go against God's orders. There remains for them that grave threat with

---

4   Allusion to the lion as symbol of divine power and revenge, e.g. in Micah 5:8, 2 Esdras 11:36-46, Revelation 5:5, and in the visions of Tobias Hess.

which we have burdened our *Fama,* and their wicked plans will rebound on their own heads. Our treasures will be left intact until the Lion shall arise, claim them for himself in his own right, accept them, and use them for the establishment of his empire.

CHAPTER SEVEN

[Reason no. 19] One thing we must confirm, O Mortals: that God has decreed that truth, light, and dignity will return to the world, soon afterward to be destroyed: such things as he ordered to leave Paradise with Adam, and to temper the misery of mankind. Thus all those lies, obscurity, and servitude will vanish, which, with the progressive instability of the great globe, have crept into the sciences, arts, and human governments, plunging them largely into darkness. [Reason no. 20] Thence were born those innumerable opinions, errors, and heresies that made it difficult even for wise men to choose. The *Fama* of the Philosophers pulled them one way, the truths of experience, the other. We trust that one day we shall see all this abolished and replaced with a single and perpetual rule. If so, we will owe our thanks to those who have worked for it, but the success of their effort will be due to the blessedness of our age.

[Reason no. 21] We acknowledge the contribution of many distinguished thinkers with their meditations on future reformation. We claim little of this glory for ourselves, as though such a task were placed on us alone. As Christ our Savior said, if there were none to carry out the divine plan, the very stones would arise and cry out.

CHAPTER EIGHT

[Reason no. 22] God's will has now sent as heralds the stars in the Serpent and the Swan, which are great signs of the great plan. They can teach how God makes these, together with human ingenuity, serve the purpose of his occult scriptures. Thus the Book of Nature is opened wide before the eyes of all, though few can either read or understand it.

[Reason no. 23] Since the human head contains two organs of hearing, two of sight, two of smell, and one of voice, it would be stupid to ask the ears to see or the eyes to hear. Thus there were ages that saw; ages that heard; and even a time of smelling. What is left, as the time is ripe and drawing to its end, is for the tongue to have its due. What once saw, heard, smelled, is now spoken. When the world awakens from the drunken sleep of its poisoned and soporific chalice, it will go to greet the rising sun with open heart, bareheaded and barefoot, merry and jubilant.

CHAPTER NINE

[Reason no. 24] Those characters and alphabet that God has inserted here and there in the Holy Bible, he has openly impressed in his admirable work of creation on the heavens, the earth, and living beings. So just as the mathematician can predict eclipses, we can foresee the dark periods of the Church and their durations. [Reason no. 25] We have derived our magic entirely from these letters, and made ourselves a new language from them that simultaneously expresses the nature of things. It is no wonder that we are less adept in other languages and in this Latin. We know that they are not in the least redolent of the Adamic or the Enochian languages, but contaminated by the confusion of Babel.

CHAPTER TEN

[Reason no. 26] While a few eagle's feathers[5] remain to delay our purpose, we must not omit the Holy Bible. We urge you to make it your one, primary, assiduous, and perpetual reading. If anyone should take delight in this, he should know that he is far advanced toward entering our Brotherhood. [Reason no. 27] This is our supreme law: that there is not one letter in such a miracle of the world that should not be pondered in the memory. The closest and most like to us are those who make a

---

5 Allusion to the double-headed eagle, emblem of the Catholic Habsburg emperors.

Bible their rule of life, the whole of their studies, the compendium of the whole world. But we insist that they not merely prattle about it, but apply it to understanding all the ages of the world; for it is not our habit to prostitute the divine oracles. The number of interpreters is endless. Some stick to one opinion for their own advantage; others practice the old trick of a making a scripture of wax that can be molded for theologians, philosophers, medics, and mathematicians alike. Our part is rather to testify that from the beginning of the world, man has been given nothing more admirable and salutary than this work, the Holy Bible. Blessed is he who owns it; more blessed, he who reads it; most blessed, he who studies it. But he who understands and serves it is most like unto God.

CHAPTER ELEVEN

[Reason no. 28] What we have said, with our loathing of impostors, against the transmutation of metals and the world's supreme medicine, we mean to be understood thus: we are far from demeaning so noble a gift of God, only it does not always bring with it the knowledge of Nature. This, on the other hand, teaches both that and innumerable other miracles of Nature. It is better for us to possess a greater understanding of philosophy, and to recommend to superior intellects not to tincture metals before they have investigated Nature. [Reason no. 29] He whom poverty, sickness, and danger cannot touch; who, thus elevated above mankind, dominates those things that torment, afflict, and grieve others, must be insatiable if he then reverts to those idle sports of building, fighting, and boasting, just because he has an inexhaustible store of gold and silver. [Reason no. 30] The supreme Ruler sees it otherwise, who exalts the humble and condemns the proud to darkness; who sends angels to discourse with the reticent, and throws the garrulous into solitude. That would be a worthy punishment of the Roman Impostor, who has vomited his abundant mouthful of blasphemies against Christ. Now in this bright light by which Germany has straightened out his tunnels and subterranean mazes, he keeps from lying, but has nonetheless filled the measure of his days and is fit for the axe. [Reason no. 31] The time will come when this viper ceases his hissing, and the triple tiara will be brought to naught. More of that when we meet.

CHAPTER TWELVE

[Reason no. 32] In concluding our Confession we must seriously urge you to discard, if not all, then most of the vile books of the pseudo-chemists. They amuse themselves by abusing the Holy Trinity for foul purposes, or deceiving men with monstrous figures and riddles. The curiosity of the credulous is their profit. Our age has produced many of this type: one of the foremost is the "Amphitheatrical" comedian,[6] a man most ingenious in deceit. The enemy of human happiness mingles such things with the good seed, to make it harder to believe the truth. Truth is simple and naked; Falsehood is specious and adorned with fringes of divine and human wisdom. [Reason no. 33] You who are prudent, flee from them and take refuge with us. We do not beg for your gold, but offer you greater treasures still. We do not lie in wait for your goods with some tale of the Tincture, but let you share in ours. We do not set you riddles, but offer you a simple and lucid explanation of the secrets. We do not ask you to invite or receive us, but call you to our houses and our more than royal palaces. This is not through any wealth of ours (in case you did not know that), but driven by the Spirit of God, commanded by the Testament of our excellent Father, and compelled by the Law of our time.

CHAPTER THIRTEEN

[Reason no. 34] What do you think, O Mortals, now that you have heard us sincerely confess Christ, execrate the Pope, earnestly embrace philosophy, lead a life worthy of a man, and invite, call, and entreat to

---

6 Allusion to Heinrich Khunrath, author of *Amphitheatrum sapientiae aeternae*, 1595.

join our community those many on whom, like us, God has shed his light? [Reason no. 35] Will you not consider it, examining your own gifts, considering how far you understand sacred Scripture, weighing the arts and counting the imperfections and shortcomings of them all? You might after all think about the remedy together with us, offer your hand to God's work, and serve the Empire of your age. [Reason no. 36] You would have the reward of this labor: all the good things that Nature has scattered over the earth would be united and brought to you as though at the center of the Sun and Moon. Then you could rid the universe of all those things that cloud human understanding and impede action, like so many eccentrics and epicycles.[7]

CHAPTER FOURTEEN

[Reason no. 37] But do not disturb our sacred silence with your clamor if you merely want to satisfy your curiosity, enticed by the gleam of gold; nor (as we would emphasize) if you are virtuous now, but could be seduced by unexpected affluence into a soft, lazy, indulgent, and complacent existence. Consider rather that, although there is a medicine that cures all ills, those whom God chooses to disturb, afflict, and punish with diseases are not given this opportunity. Although we could instruct and educate the whole world and free it from endless troubles, we are not made known to anyone unless God permits it. It is impossible for anyone to enjoy our benefits against God's will. He will sooner lose his life in searching for us than attain felicity by finding us.

—The Brotherhood of the R.C.

---

[7] The hypothetical circular movements introduced to explain planetary orbits, especially in the geocentric system.

III.
THE CHEMICAL WEDDING OF CHRISTIAN ROSENKREUZ IN THE YEAR 1459

by Johann Valentin Andreae

Translated from the German edition of 1616, with an introduction by Joscelyn Godwin

With twenty-eight pen drawings by Hans Wildermann

Introduction to the *Chemical Wedding*

Recent scholarship, especially that of Carlos Gilly and Roland Edighoffer,[1] has clarified the beginnings of the Rosicrucian movement as never before. This makes it possible to introduce the *Chemical Wedding of Christian Rosenkreuz*[2] by placing it within the context of Johann Valentin Andreae's own life, writings, and perhaps motives.

During his student years at Tübingen University (1601–1605), the precocious Andreae wrote a number of original works, including political and astrological tracts. Most relevantly, he also wrote two plays inspired by the English theatrical groups that toured in the German-speaking lands. Either then or during his spell as a private tutor (1607), he wrote a short novel or comedy called *Chymische Hochzeit* (Chemical Wedding). He invented for it the character of Christian Rosenkreuz, whose name is a play on the Andreae family's coat of arms: a saltire, or Saint Andrew's cross, between four red roses. The wedding in question is not Christian's own but that of a fairytale king and queen. He is chosen to assist in the process, which includes the beheading of the royal couple and their resurrection through chemical, or rather alchemical operations—an interest that Andreae shared with his father. This early work remained unpublished, and no copy of it is known.

Between 1609 and 1611, Andreae traveled in various French-speaking lands. Especially after seeing the high level of public morality in Calvinist Geneva, he developed a vision of how an ideal Christian society might work. It would be free from the sectarian divisions that were already threatening to tear Europe apart. Following the principles

---
1 See notes 11 and 12 to the Introduction to the *Fama*.
2 In view of the various early spellings of the name (Rosenkreutz, Rosencreütz, etc.), we use the now standard spelling based on the modern German *Kreuz*, "cross."

of Paracelsus's *Theophrastia Sacra* (see Introduction to the *Fama*, p. 5), it would combine the study of the Bible with that of the natural world, as being God's two revelations.

Around 1610, Andreae applied his gift for fiction to this ideal, writing another tale of his alter ego but giving Christian Rosenkreuz a history and character entirely at variance with the previous one. This was the basis for the *Fama*, which, on Andreae's return, he shared with a few like-minded friends. With their collaboration, he developed that and the *Confessio* as the imaginary manifestos of an imaginary brotherhood. Copies were made, and soon escaped to multiply beyond the group's control. So fascinating was the story of Rosenkreuz's travels in the East, his foundation of a brotherhood, secret burial, and the rediscovery of his elaborate tomb, so attractive the summons to join that elect society, that many readers took it literally. In 1612, as we have read, Adam Haslmayr published the first response to it, which greatly increased public interest.

Early in 1614, Landgraf Moritz of Hesse authorized the printing of the *Fama*. Since the authorship was as yet unknown, no one sought Andreae's permission. The title page served anti-Catholic propaganda by mentioning that because of his response, Haslmayr had been arrested by the Jesuits and put in irons as a galley slave. (This was true; in 1614 he was in the middle of his five-year sentence.) The appearance of the *Fama*, and soon after that of the *Confessio*, was a surprise to Andreae. His Rosenkreuz stories already lay in the past, and his mind was on other things altogether. In 1612 or 1613, he had made a long trip to Italy. Back in Tübingen, he and Christoph Besold had been pursuing their scientific interests, holding a "Collegium Mathematicum" which dealt in the practical applications of mathematics, and Andreae had published an illustrated mathematical book.[3] In 1614 he married, and took up his first official church post as pastor in Vaihingen, near Stuttgart. He also became a correspondent and admirer of Johann

---

3 *Collectaneorum Mathematicorum Decades XI. Centum et decem tabulis Aeneis exhibitae* (Tübingen: Johann Alexander Cellius, 1614).

Arndt (1555–1621), a prominent Lutheran theologian and an inspiration to the later movement of Pietism. Andreae would translate some of Arndt's work into Latin, and make it the basis for his own Christian utopia, the *Republic of Christianopolis* (published 1619). Somehow he found time to write a counterpart to the hundred newsletters of Boccalini's *Ragguagli di Parnaso*: a hundred satirical dialogues on the stupidities of his time, under the title *Menippus*.[4]

What follows is more conjectural. In 1615, half amused, half worried by the furore that the Rosicrucian myth had unleashed, Andreae went back to his early fantasy. How much of it he rewrote depends on whether he had already known Boccaccio's tales and Francesco Colonna's *Hypnerotomachia Poliphili*, for the *Chemical Wedding*, as published, repeats some of Boccaccio's stories and is suffused with memories of Colonna's epic novel.[5] If Andreae had not read the *Hypnerotomachia* in its original language, he might well have read it in French, either in the Kerver edition of 1546 or the abridgment by Béroalde de Verville, which included an alchemical interpretation.[6] In any case, the *Chemical Wedding* bears every sign of later polishing and improvement, both literary and mathematical.[7] Carlos Gilly relates the next stage of its publication:

> We do not know whether the printing of the *Chymische Hochzeit* in Strassburg was with Andreae's consent. Nonetheless, the editor was the well-known engraver and Arndt pupil Johann Friedrich Jung of Strassburg, who in an *Epistola an die Fratres Rosae Crucis*

---

[4] See Thomas Willard, "Andreae's *ludibrium*: Menippean Satire in the *Chymische Hochzeit*," in Albrecht Classen, ed., *Laughter in the Middle Ages and Early Modern Times* (Berlin: De Gruyter, 2010), pp. 767–789.
[5] For some parallels, see Efthymia Priki, "Elucidating and Enigmatizing: The Reception of the *Hypnerotomachia Poliphili* in the Early Modern Period and in the Twentieth and Twenty-First Centuries," eSharp 14 (2009), pp. 62–90 (accessed online).
[6] François Béroalde de Verville, *Le Tableau des riches inventions, couvertes du voile des fêtes amoureuses, qui sont présentées dans le Songe de Poliphile* (Paris: Matthieu Guillemot, 1600).
[7] As Adam McLean's analysis shows, it is structured at every level by the number seven. See Adam McLean's commentary in *The Chemical Wedding of Christian Rosenkreuz*, trans. Joscelyn Godwin (Grand Rapids: Phanes Press, 1991), pp. 113–22.

dated December 3, 1615, announced the work as follows: "As I ended this letter, I was given for review a short German book with the title *Nyptiae Chymicae,* or *Chymische Hochzeit Christiani Rosenkreutz im Jahre 1459,* without a doubt written by the first Brother and Founder of your Order. The entire alchemical art is described enigmatically, which pleased me so much that I answered my employer: the book is absolutely worth printing, even though it will not lack for envy and mockery."[8]

Since there is no sign of the *Chemical Wedding* having leaked out before its publication as the *Fama* had been, I suspect that Andreae himself gave it, in its revised form, to Jung or to the publisher, Zetzner. It certainly served a triple purpose. As mentioned, the Christian Rosenkreuz of the novel shares only his name with "our father Christian" of the *Fama* and *Confessio.* He is an old hermit of no distinction, no universal knowledge (compare Reason no. 8 of the *Confessio*), with no brotherhood around him. Since he is so obviously a fictional character, then it stands to reason that the C.R.C. of the manifestos was no more,[9] and that it was foolish to take them seriously. On the positive side, the narrator of the *Chemical Wedding* is a moral exemplar whose signal virtue is humility; he does not think of himself as special, and admits his ignorance at every point. After his bizarre experiences, he returns home to his simple, pious life. That is the second level of instruction. Thirdly, the events he witnesses are an allegory of spiritual alchemy, with death and resurrection as the crucial, and Christian, requisites for the marriage of soul and spirit.

On the title page of the *Chemical Wedding,* a conspicuous Latin inscription reads, "Published secrets become valueless, and things profaned lose their grace. Therefore cast not pearls before swine, nor strew roses before an ass." It could be read as a reproach to the publication

---

8   Gilly, *Cimelia Rhodostaurotica,* pp. 82–83.
9   As if it were not suspicious that C.R.C. was interred in 1484 with a book by Paracelsus, who was not yet born.

of the *Fama* and *Confessio,* private utopian manifestos over which so many had made asses of themselves. A. E. Waite comments, "But the author of these lines—whom I do not claim to identify—had forgotten Apuleius and his Golden Ass."[10] What if he had not, and knowingly coupled the Apuleian allusion with Jesus' image of casting pearls before swine?[11] For it was through eating red roses that Lucius, the narrator of *Metamorphoses, or The Golden Ass,* was restored from donkey to human form, and went on to initiation into the mysteries of Isis and Osiris. The irony of the inscription is that the *Chemical Wedding,* with its alchemical secrets, *was* being published now, strewing its roses for each to take according to his ability.

The translation that follows revises and corrects my previous version of 1991 (see note 7 above). The latter remains indispensable for esoteric students because of Adam McLean's fifty-page commentary and the addition of the *Parabola* of Hinrichus Madathanus. These are omitted here, the present intention being not to interpret but to provide a modern English text for readers of all interests and persuasions. I thank Franziska Goetzke of the Albert-Ludwigs-Universität, Freiburg im Breisgau, for reviewing my translation, but any faults that remain are my own.

Despite extensive researches, we have unfortunately not been able to determine the holder of the rights to the drawings by Hans Wildermann, which are reproduced here. They were first published in 1923, in a bibliophiles' edition of the work.[12] The text was set in Gothic type, with capitals and marginalia in red. Hans Wilhelm Wildermann (1884–1954) was a prolific sculptor, painter, scene designer, and illustrator, especially of religious, romantic, and musical subjects. These twenty-eight pen

---

10 A.E. Waite, *The Brotherhood of the Rosy Cross* (New Hyde Park: University Books, n.d.; first ed. 1924), p. 159.
11 Matthew 7:6.
12 *Chymische Hochzeit Christiani Rosenkreutz anno Domini MCCCCLIX. Verfasst von Joh. Val. Andreae. Mit achtundzwanzig Federzeichnungen von Hans Wildermann* (Regensburg: Gustav Bosse Verlag, 1923). Vol. 5 in the series "Regensburger Liebhaberdrucke."

drawings are, to my knowledge, the most complete cycle of illustrations of the *Chemical Wedding*.[13] Their delicacy and humor remind us that Andreae's novel, however profound, is still a comedy. Like the plays that Shakespeare was writing around the same time (*Cymbeline, The Winter's Tale, The Tempest*), or the serio-comic alchemical works of Michael Maier (*Lusus serius, Jocus severus*), it conveys deep truths with a light touch.

---

13 Seven major drawings and several smaller ones by Johfra Bosschart (1919–1998) illustrate the translation of the *Chemical Wedding* (from the Dutch) in Jan Van Rijckenborgh, *The Secrets of the Brotherhood of the Rosycross: Esoteric Analysis of the Spiritual Testament of the Order of the Rosycross* (Haarlem: Rozekruis Pers, 1991).

The Chemical Wedding of Christian Rosenkreuz

THE FIRST DAY

ONE EVENING before Easter I was sitting at table, having, as was my habit, finished my humble prayer to my Creator, and meditated on the many great mysteries which the Father of Light, in his majesty, had allowed me to glimpse. As I was trying to prepare inwardly a pure unleavened loaf to accompany my blessed Paschal Lamb, there suddenly arose such a terrific wind that I thought the mountain on which my cottage was built was going to split apart. However, I was accustomed to this kind of thing and to other tricks of the Devil, who had done me many an injury; so I took courage and remained in my meditation until, quite against expectation, someone tapped me on the back. I was so alarmed by this that I scarcely dared to turn around; yet I showed as much composure as human frailty can in such a plight. But when something pulled at my coat several times, I looked round.

There stood a wonderfully beautiful female figure, dressed all in blue, spangled like the heavens with golden stars. In her right hand she held a large trumpet all of gold, on which a name was engraved which I could plainly read, but am forbidden to reveal as yet. In her left hand she held a great bundle of letters in all languages, which, as I later learnt, she was to take to every land. She also had huge and lovely wings, studded all over with eyes, so that she could take off and fly swifter than any eagle. I might well have noticed more about her if her visit had not been so brief, and if I had not been so filled with terror and astonishment, but there I must leave it. For as soon as I turned around, she leafed here and there through her letters and at last pulled out a small note, laying it on the table with deep reverence and leaving me without a single word. As she flew up, she blew so loudly on her golden trumpet that the whole mountain echoed with it, and for nearly a quarter of an hour I could scarcely hear my own voice.

THE CHEMICAL WEDDING OF CHRISTIAN ROSENKREUZ

Poor fellow that I was, I did not know what to think or do in the face of such an unexpected adventure; so I fell on my knees and prayed my Creator not to let anything happen to imperil my eternal salvation. Then with fear and trembling I turned to the letter which could scarcely have weighed more if it had been made from solid gold. As I examined it carefully, I found it closed with a small seal on which was engraved a delicate cross and the motto: *In hoc signo* ✝ *vinces* [In this sign ✝ you will conquer].

I was much relieved when I saw this sign, for I knew that the Devil could not stand such a seal, much less use it. So I carefully opened the letter, and found written there, with golden letters on a blue ground, the following verse:

> Today—today—today
> Is the wedding of the King.
> If you are born for this,
> Chosen by God for joy,
> You may ascend the mount
> Whereon three temples stand
> And see the thing yourself.
>
> Take heed,
> Observe yourself!
> If you are not washed clean,
> The wedding can work ill.
> Perjure here at your peril;
> He who is light, beware!

And at the bottom it said: *Sponsus et Sponsa* [Bridegroom and Bride]. As I read this letter, I nearly fainted away, my hair stood on end, and cold sweat ran down over my whole body. Although I recognized that this was the promised wedding about which I had been told in a bodily vision seven years before, the one I had awaited so long and with such yearning, and carefully planned and calculated from my planetary tables, I would never have expected it to take place under such difficult and dangerous conditions. Originally I had thought that I would merely have to appear at the wedding to be a welcome guest; but now I was referred to divine Providence, of which up to now I was never certain.

Looking at myself, the more I pondered, I could see that there was nothing in my head but a great want of sense and a blindness in secret matters. And if I could not even grasp the things that lay beneath my feet, which I dealt with every day, how much less was I born for the investigation and discovery of nature's secrets! In my opinion, nature could surely have found a better pupil to entrust with her precious treasure, however temporal and transient it may be.

I also found that my physical life, outward conduct, and brotherly love toward my neighbor were far from being purged and pure enough. I was aware of fleshly desires, which aim only for reputation and worldly show, not for the well-being of others; I was always thinking how I could use my skills for my own immediate benefit, for building splendid things, for making an everlasting name in the world, and other such materialistic thoughts. But what troubled me most were the dark words about the three temples, which I could not understand for all my cogitation, and would not understand even today if they had not been miraculously revealed to me. As I trembled now in fear and hope, my thoughts straying hither and thither but especially over my weakness and incompetence, knowing no way to help myself and thoroughly unsettled by this summons, I resorted at last to my tried and trusty practice: I lay down in my bed after praying long and earnestly that my good angel might appear to me through God's grace and help me in this perplexity, as had sometimes happened before. And so it turned out, to God's glory, for my good, and for the sake of my neighbor, as a true and sincere warning and betterment.

Scarcely had I fallen asleep, when it seemed to me that I was lying in a great dark tower with countless other people, bound in heavy

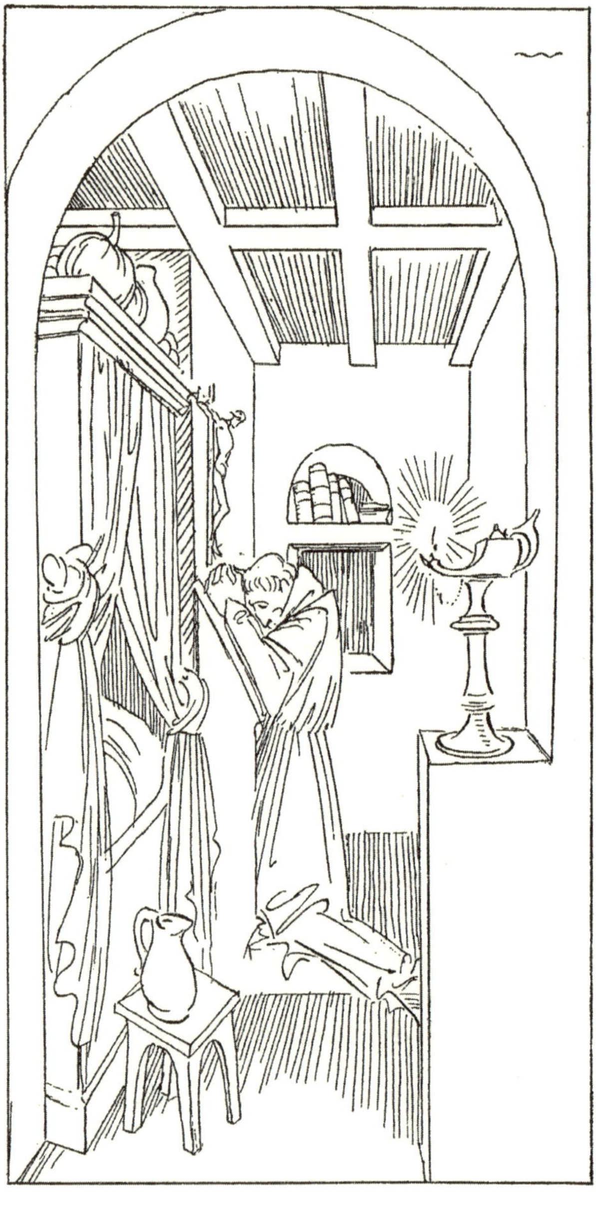

chains. There was no light, and we were crawling over one another like bees, thus increasing each other's suffering. Although neither I nor anyone else could see a single thing, I could hear when one person heaved himself over another, when his chains or fetters became the slightest bit lighter, although none had much to gain by this, since we were all captive wretches.

After I and the others had continued a good while in this misery, continually rebuking one another for our blindness and captivity, at last we heard the sound of many trumpets. Kettledrums rolled, too, so majestically that even in our torment we felt aroused and quickened. As the music played, the ceiling of the tower opened and a little light was let in to us. Then we could all be seen tumbling over each other in confusion, though if one person heaved himself up too high, he would fall under the others' feet. In short, everyone wanted to be on top, and I was no exception. Despite my heavy fetters I pressed forward with the rest and clambered up onto a stone which I had spied. Though others often grabbed at me, I defended myself with hands and feet as well as I could. We had no other thought than that we should all be set free.

But this was by no means the case. For after the authorities, who looked down on us through the gap above, had enjoyed for a while our sprawlings and moanings, a gray-haired old man ordered us to be silent, and as the noise died away began to speak, as I still remember it:

> If it would not struggle so,
> The wretched human race,
> Many a good would come to it
> From my mother's store.
> But no: since it will not obey,
> It still remains in misery
> > And must be locked up.

Yet would my mother dear
Not look upon its sin;
She lets her precious gifts
Abundantly appear,
Although this seldom happens,
So that they have some worth
      And are not thought a fable.
To celebrate the festival
Which we hold today,
To make her mercy known,
A good work she will do.
The rope will now come down:
Whoever can hang on,
      The same shall be set free.

Scarcely had he spoken these words than the old woman ordered her servants to let down the rope into the tower seven times, and to haul out those who hung onto it. Goodness! If I could only describe the excitement that seized us: everyone tried to snatch the rope, thereby hindering everyone else. But after seven minutes a sign was given by a small bell, at which the servants pulled out four of us. I could not possibly reach the rope, since, as I have said, I was perched to my great distress on a stone in the wall of the tower, and hence could not touch the rope which hung down in the middle. A second time the rope was let down. Many people's chains were too heavy, their hands too weak, so that they could not hold onto it; but as they fell they knocked down many others who might have been able to hang on. Many were actually pulled off by ones who could not reach it themselves, so that in our great distress they grew furious with one another. But I most pitied those who were so heavy that they could not rise, though their hands were torn from their bodies.

Thus it went, so that after five attempts only a few had been pulled out; for as soon as the sign was given, the servants were so quick at hauling that most people tumbled off again, and the fifth time the rope was pulled up quite empty. Hence almost everyone despaired of rescue, myself included, and cried to God to have pity on us and release us from this darkness. He must have heard some of us, for as the rope came down for the sixth time, a few hung strongly onto it. As it rose, it swung from side to side and happened, perhaps through God's will, to swing toward me. I quickly grabbed it, sat on top of all the others, and thus beyond all expectation I finally came out. Such was my joy that I took no heed of a wound in my head, caused by a sharp stone as I was pulled up, until I and the other freed prisoners had helped (as all had done before) with the seventh and last pull. Then I first realized that the effort had made my blood flow all over my clothes, having completely overlooked it in my joy.

Now after the last pull, which brought up the most people, the woman had the rope laid aside and told her exceedingly aged son (which astonished me) to tell the other prisoners their sentence. After brief consideration, he spoke up thus:

> Beloved children,
> Who are here,
> It is fulfilled
> That long was known,
> Which my mother's great pity
> Has bestowed on you.
> You should not take it in bad part;
> A blessed time will soon be yours,
> When all men shall be equals,
> And none be rich or poor.
> Those charged with much

Must produce much.
Those entrusted with much
Will be kept hard at it.
So cease your great bewailing!
It will last but a few days.

As soon as these words were spoken, the roof was replaced and locked, and the trumpets and kettledrums started up again. But loud though the music was, one could still hear the bitter laments of the prisoners coming from the tower; it soon brought the tears to my own eyes.

Thereupon the old woman sat down with her son on the seats prepared for them, and ordered for the released prisoners to be counted. When the count was done and written on a golden-yellow tablet, she asked each one's name, which was likewise written down by a page boy. As she looked at each of us, she sighed and spoke to her son, so that I could hear: "Ah, how I sorrow for the poor people in the tower! Would God that I could free them all!" Whereupon her son answered: "Mother, it is ordered thus by God, and we must not strive against it. What if we were all lords, and possessed all the goods of earth, and were sitting at table: who would bring us our food?"

At this, the mother was silent a while, then she said: "Well, let these ones be freed from their fetters," and it was quickly done. I was almost the last, yet I could not restrain myself, though I was still watching the others, from bowing down before the old woman and thanking God, my loving father, who through her had brought me out of such darkness and into the light. Others did likewise, and the woman bowed in reply.

At last each was given a gold medal as a commemoration and as provision. One side was stamped with the rising sun; the other, as far as I remember, with these three letters: D.L.S. *(Deus Lux Solis; Deo Laus Semper)* [God, the light of the sun; Praise always to God]. Then each was

THE CHEMICAL WEDDING OF CHRISTIAN ROSENKREUZ

given leave to go about his business, with the charge to serve God's glory and help our neighbor, and to guard in silence what was confided to us. This we promised, and parted from one another. But I, because of the wounds made by the fetters, found it hard going and limped with both feet. As soon as the old woman saw this, she laughed at it and called me back, saying: "My son, do not let this flaw distress you, but remember your faults and thank God that he has allowed you to attain so high a light while still in this world and in all your imperfection; and bear these wounds for my sake."

Thereupon the trumpets started up again, startling me so that I awoke. Then for the first time I realized that it had only been a dream. But it remained so strongly in my mind that it still troubled me, and I seemed still to feel the wounds on my feet. From all this I concluded that I was invited by God to attend this secret and occult wedding. Wherefore I thanked the divine Majesty with childlike trust, and prayed that he might keep me in his fear, fill my heart daily with wisdom and understanding, and at last bring me through his mercy to the desired goal, undeserving though I was.

Thereupon I prepared for my journey. I put on my white linen coat, and girded myself with a blood-red belt bound crosswise over my shoulders. In my hat I stuck four red roses, so that I could be more easily recognized in the crowd by this sign. For provisions I took bread, salt, and water, following the advice of one who knew, which in the event proved very fortunate. But before I stepped out of my cottage, I fell on my knees in this outfit and wedding-garment and prayed God that whatever might happen, he would bring it to a good end. Then I vowed in the sight of God that I would use everything that might be revealed to me through his grace, not for honor or prestige in the world, but only for the glory of his name and the service of my fellow men. With this vow and with high hopes I departed from my hermitage with joy.

THE SECOND DAY

As soon as I had I left my hermitage and reached the forest, it seemed to me as if the whole heavens and all the elements were already decked out for this wedding. For even the birds, I thought, sang more sweetly than usual, and the young fawns gamboled around so happily that my old heart was warmed, and, moved to song, I began to sing loudly:

> Dear little bird, rejoice,
> And loudly praise your maker,
> Let your voice ring bright and clear;
> Your God is high above.
> He has prepared your food
> And gives it in due season,
>   So therefore be contented.
> Why should you be sorrowful,
> Why should you rail at God?
> Because he's made you just a bird
> Don't let it turn your head.
> If he has not made you a man
> Be still: he has done well thereby,
>   So therefore be contented.
> How should I do, poor earthworm,
> To argue with my God,
> As if I had the power to fight
> The very storm of heaven?
> God will not be resisted thus:
> If you think otherwise, begone!
>   Man, therefore be contented.
> That he's not made you Emperor,
> Should be no grief to you.

> Perhaps you took his name in vain;
> He is aware of this.
> The eyes of God are sharp and keen,
> He sees into your heart.
>> Thus God is not deceived.

I sang this song with all my heart, so that it resounded through the forest and the last words echoed back to me from the mountain, until at length I caught sight of a pleasant green meadow and stepped out of the forest. On this meadow stood three tall and splendid cedar trees, which were so broad as to cast a lovely, welcome shadow. I was delighted by this, for although I had not come far, my great yearning was making me exhausted. So I hurried up to the trees, to rest a little beneath them.

As I approached, I perceived a tablet fastened to one of the trees. After a while I read on it the following words, written in elegant script:[1]

> Hail, guest! If you should have heard the news of the King's wedding, then hearken to these words. The Bridegroom bids us offer you the choice of four paths, by all of which you may reach the royal castle, if you do not fall by the wayside.
>
> The first is short but perilous, and will lead you through rocky places from which you may scarcely escape.
>
> The second is longer, and will lead you not downward but round and round; it is flat and easy, so long as you have the aid of a magnet and do not let yourself be diverted to right or left.
>
> The third is truly the Royal Way, which will make your journey delightful with various pleasures and spectacles of our realm. But hitherto scarcely one in a thousand has achieved it.
>
> By the fourth way, no man may come to the kingdom, for it is a consuming path and suited only to incorruptible bodies.
>
> Choose now which of the three you wish, and be constant thereon. But know that whichever you have taken, it is destined

---

[1] In the original, this inscription is in Latin.

THE CHEMICAL WEDDING OF CHRISTIAN ROSENKREUZ

to you by immutable Fate, and you may go back on it only at the greatest peril of your life.

This is what we would have you know. But hearken to this warning: you do not know how much danger you incur on this way. If you are guilty of the slightest offence against the laws of our King, I beseech you to turn back while you still may, and return swiftly home by the way you came.

As soon as I had read this inscription, all my joy left me again, and I, who had been singing so cheerfully up to now, began to weep bitterly. I could see clearly the three paths before me, and knew that I would be allowed to choose one of them when the time came. But I was afraid that I would hit upon the rocky and craggy path, and fall to a miserable death. Or, if the long path were my lot, I would either lose my way or be left behind on the long journey. Of course I could not hope to be the one in a thousand who chooses the Royal Way. I could also see the fourth path before me, but it was enveloped in such fire and steam that I dared not even venture near it. So I reflected in my mind whether I should turn back, or choose one of the paths for myself. I was painfully aware of my unworthiness, but comforted myself with the dream in which I had been rescued from the tower. At the same time, I felt that I should not let a mere dream make me complacent; and so my thoughts went round and round, until in my great weariness my belly cried out from hunger and thirst. So I drew out my bread and cut it up.

Just then I saw a snow-white dove perched on the tree, which I had not noticed before. It fluttered down quite naturally, as perhaps it was used to doing, and approached me without fear. I gladly offered it a share of my food, which it accepted, cheering me somewhat with its beauty. But as soon as the dove's enemy, a black raven, spied it, it hurtled down upon the dove, taking no notice of me, and tried to seize its food, so that the dove's only defense lay in flight. The two birds both flew off to the South, which so angered and troubled me that I hurried thoughtlessly after the evil raven, unintentionally running nearly a field's length along one of the paths, driving off the raven and freeing the dove.

Immediately I realized how thoughtlessly I had acted; I had already taken one of the paths, and now I dared not go back on it for fear of terrible reprisals. To some extent I could put up with that, but I was most upset to have left my bag and bread behind by the tree, and to be unable to fetch them. For no sooner did I turn around than a powerful gale met me and blew me over; yet when I went forward on the path I felt nothing at all. This was enough to convince me that it would cost me my life to try to oppose the wind. So I patiently took up my cross, got to my feet, and determined to do my utmost to reach the goal before nightfall.

There appeared to be many byways, but thanks to my compass I avoided them. I turned not a foot's breadth from the meridian, although the path was sometimes so rough and unkempt that I was quite unsure of it. On the way I thought constantly of the dove and the raven, but could not fathom their meaning. Finally I spied from a distance, on a high mountain, a splendid portal. I hastened toward this, although it lay distant and far from the path, because the sun had already sunk beneath the mountains and I could descry no other refuge. All this I attribute solely to God, who could very well have let me continue on my way, and could have shielded my eyes so that I would have missed this portal. So I hurried on, as I said, with all speed, and reached the gate while there was still daylight enough to see it.

It was an altogether fair and royal portal, carved with many wonderful images and objects, each of which, as I later discovered, had its peculiar meaning. At the top was a largish tablet with the inscription: *Procul hinc, procul ite prophani!* [Away, away from here, profane ones!], and other things which it is strictly forbidden me to tell. As soon as I stepped beneath it, out came a porter clothed in sky-blue. I gave him a friendly greeting which he returned, then he immediately demanded my letter of invitation.

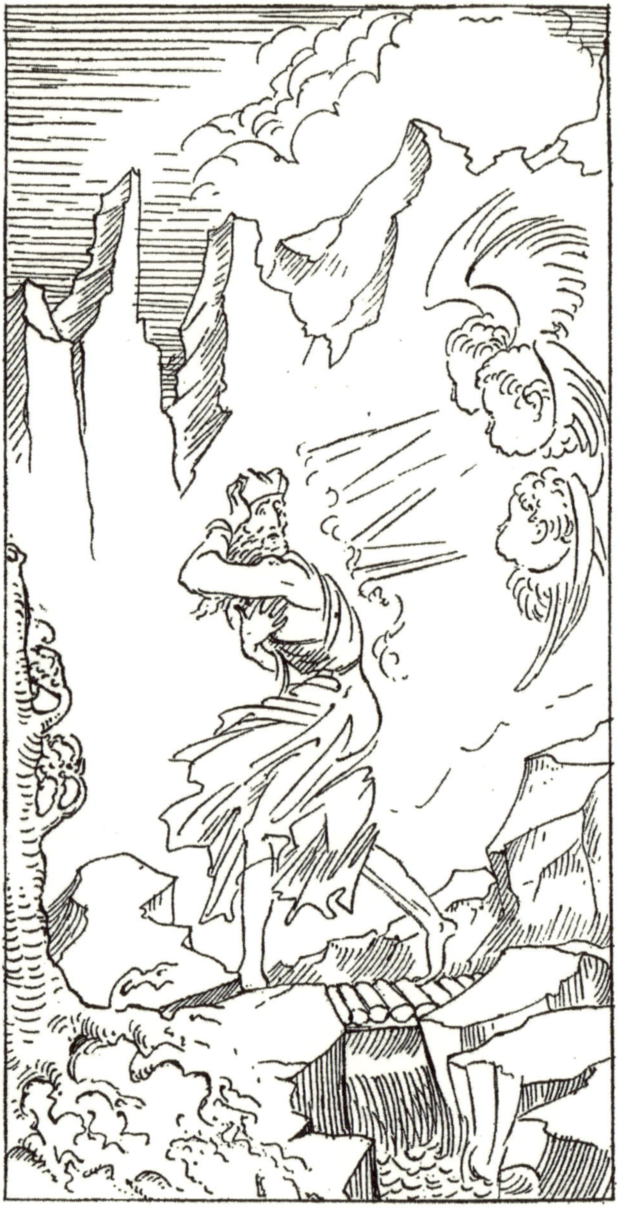

Oh, how glad I was that I had brought it with me! For how easily I might have forgotten it, as had indeed happened to others, so he told me. I quickly drew it out, and he was not only satisfied but to my amazement showed me great respect, saying: "Go ahead, my brother; you are my welcome guest!" Then he asked my name, and when I answered that I was a brother of the Red Rose Cross, he was both surprised and delighted. Then he went on: "My brother, have you nothing with you to exchange for a token?" I replied that my means were scanty, but that if he liked anything that I had with me, he was welcome to it. He requested my small water bottle, and gave me in exchange a golden token on which was nothing but the two letters: S.C. *(Sanctitate constantia; Sponsus charus; Spes charitas)* [Constant in holiness; Beloved husband; Hope, charity].

The porter asked me that if this should become useful, I would remember him. Thereupon I asked him how many had gone in before me, which he also told me. Finally he gave me, out of friendship, a sealed note for the second porter.

As I tarried a little longer with him, night fell. A great pan of pitch was lit above the gate, so that if anyone were still on the way they could hasten toward it. But the road that led on to the castle was closed in on both sides by high walls and planted with all sorts of beautiful fruit trees. On every third tree lanterns were hung, which had been lit by a beautiful maiden, dressed likewise in blue, with a bright torch. It was so splendid and artistic to behold that I lingered more than I should have. But eventually, after I had learned enough and received useful advice from him, I took friendly leave of the first porter.

As I continued, I would have loved to know what my letter said; but since I could expect nothing unfriendly of the porter, I had to repress my curiosity and put the path behind me until I came to the second portal. This was almost identical to the first one, only with different images and decorations of mysterious meaning. The tablet attached to it read: *Date et dabitur vobis* [Give, and it shall be given to you]. Beneath this portal a frightful lion lay chained, which immediately jumped up when it saw me and came at me with a loud roar. Thereupon the second porter, who had been lying on a slab of marble, awoke and told me not to fear or fret. He drove the lion behind him and took the note, which I reached out to him with trembling hand, read it, and spoke with great reverence: "Now by God's grace is come the man whom I have long wished to see!" He also took out a token and asked me if I could redeem it. Having nothing left but my salt, I offered him that, and he accepted it with thanks. Once more, the medal bore only two letters: S.M. *(Studio merentis; Sal humor* [sic]*; Sponso mittendus; Sal mineralis; Sal menstrualis)* [By studying the worthy; Humor salt; Pledge for the Bridegroom; Mineral Salt; Menstrual Salt].

Just as I was trying to speak with this porter, bells began to ring from within the castle. He urged me to hurry, lest all my trouble and labor be in vain; for they were already beginning to extinguish the lights above. So quickly did I obey that in my anxiety I forgot to take leave of the porter. It was high time, for as fast as I ran, the maiden was just behind me, and all the lights were going out behind her. I could never have found my way if she had not cast some light with her torch. It was all I could do to slip in just as she did, then the door was slammed so violently that a bit of my coat was caught in it. Naturally I had to leave it behind, for neither I nor those who were already calling outside the door could persuade the guard to open it again. He swore that he had given the keys to the maiden, and that she had taken them with her into the court.

Meanwhile I looked round again at the portal. The whole world has nothing to compare with it for richness. Flanking the door were two columns: on one stood a cheerful statue with the inscription *Congratulor* [I congratulate], while the other veiled its face and looked sorrowful, and beneath it was written *Condoleo* [I condole]. In short, there were such dark and mysterious sayings and images on it, that the most learned man on

THE CHEMICAL WEDDING OF CHRISTIAN ROSENKREUZ

earth could not have expounded them. But if God will permit, I shall soon publish and explain them all.

At this portal I had to give my name again. It was written down as the last one in a small parchment book, and delivered with others to the Lord Bridegroom. Then at last I was given the proper guest token, a little smaller than the others, but far heavier, on which were these letters: S.P.N. *(Salus per Naturam; Sponsi praesentandus nuptiis)* [Salvation through Nature; To be presented to the Bridegroom at the wedding]. I was also given a new pair of shoes, since the floor of the castle was inlaid with pure polished marble. My old ones I was to give to one of the poor men who sat beneath the porch in great numbers, but very orderly. So I gave them to an old man. Two pages with torches[2] now led me to a small room. There they told me to sit down on a bench, which I did. They extinguished their torches in two holes in the floor, and went away leaving me sitting all alone. Soon after, I heard a noise but saw nothing: it was some men stumbling over me, but since I could not see, I had to put up with it and await what they would do. I soon realized that they were barbers, so I begged them not to push me about so; I would willingly do whatever they wanted. Thereupon they let me go, and one, whom I still could not see, cut off the hair very neatly round the top of my head, but left my long gray hair in place over my forehead, eyes, and ears. In this first encounter, I must admit, I was quite desperate, since they shoved me so hard while I was unable to see; I could only think that God was making me suffer for my curiosity. But now these invisible barbers dutifully gathered up the fallen hair and went off with it, whereupon the two pages returned and laughed heartily at me for having been so frightened.

We had scarcely exchanged a few words when someone started ringing a little bell again, which the pages told me was the signal for assembly. They invited me to follow them, and lit my way through many passages,

---

2   The text reads *Ein Knab, mit zweyen Fackeln*, that is, "One page, with two torches." However, the following verbs are plural and later two pages are mentioned.

doors, and spiral stairs, as far as a great hall. Inside was a large crowd of guests: Emperors, Kings, lords and gentlemen, noble and common, rich and poor, and all manner of people, which surprised me greatly so that I thought to myself: "Oh, what a big fool you've been, to have let yourself in for such a disagreeable journey! Look: those are people you know very well and have never thought much of. They are already here, but you, for all your pleading and praying, came in last by the skin of your teeth." This and more the Devil put into my head, though I did my best to show him the door. Meanwhile my acquaintances spoke to me, now one, now another, saying: "Well, well, Brother Rosenkreuz, are you here too?" "Indeed, my brethren," I answered, "God's grace has helped me come here, too." They found this very laughable, thinking it silly to need God's help for so slight a thing. I had just asked one of them about his journey (for most of them had had to climb over the rocks), when some trumpets, none of which we could see, began to summon us to table. They all sat down, each one in whatever place he thought set him above the others. I and a few other poor souls were scarcely left a little room at the lowest table. The two pages entered, and one of them said such a beautiful and uplifting grace as to warm my heart. But a few louts took little notice of this, laughing and winking at each other, biting their hats, and similar fooleries. Then the food was brought in, and although not a person was to be seen, everything was managed so well that it seemed as if each guest had his own server. As soon as my clever friends were a little refreshed, and the wine had taken away their inhibitions, the boasting began, at which they were very good. One would dare this, another that, while the most useless idiots generally bragged the loudest. When I think about the impossible and preternatural things I heard there, even today I get indignant about it. Finally they could no longer keep to their places, but one toady would be thrusting himself among the lords here, another there. They boasted of such deeds as neither Samson nor Hercules could have achieved, for all their strength. One wanted to relieve Atlas of his burden, another to fetch three-headed Cerberus out of Hell again. In short, each one had his own squadron, and the great lords were so stupid as to believe their pretensions. In the end, the scoundrels got very bold, not caring though a few got their knuckles rapped with knives, and when one happened to filch a golden chain, they all wanted to try it.

I saw one who could hear the sound of the heavens; another who could see the Platonic Ideas; a third would number the atoms of Democritus. Quite a few had discovered perpetual motion. Some seemed to me quite intelligent, but spoiled it by thinking too highly of themselves. Finally, there was one who would have us believe then and there that he could see the servants waiting on us, and he would have taken his insolence further, had not one of the invisible servers dealt him such a blow on his lying mouth that not only he, but many around him, fell silent as mice.

What gave me most satisfaction was that all the people I had any regard for were perfectly quiet in their conduct and made no outcry, but, aware of their lack of understanding, regarded Nature's secrets as far too high, and themselves as far too low.

In this tumult, I was close to ruing the day that had brought me here. It was painful to see how loose and wanton types sat at the table above, while I was not even left in peace in my little corner, but one of these oafs called me a fool in motley. I did not know at the time that there was still one portal to be passed, but thought that I would have to spend the whole wedding thus mocked, scorned, and humiliated. I had never done anything to deserve this, either from the Bridegroom or from his Bride; in my opinion, he should have found another fool than I to invite to his wedding. One can see from this what discontent this world's inequities can bring to simple souls. But it was actually a part of my lameness, of which I had dreamed.

The general clamor got steadily louder. There were some who boasted of false and spurious visions, and wanted to tell us of palpably lying dreams. However, there sat near me a quiet and refined man who spoke now and then of better things. Finally he said to me: "Look, brother, if someone were to come and try to bring such hardened sinners onto the right path, do you think they would listen to him?"

"Certainly not," I replied.

"Perhaps the world wants to be deceived," said he, "and will not listen to those who wish it well. Just look at that toady: with what crazy talk and idiotic thoughts he seduces others to him! And that one there, who fools people with words of wonder and mystery. Believe me, though, the time will come when these liars will have the masks ripped from their faces, and the whole world will know what swindlers of the people lurk beneath. Then perhaps the neglected will be honored."

As he spoke thus, with the clamor becoming worse the longer it went on, there suddenly arose in the hall such a lovely and stately music as I had never heard in my life before. All fell silent in expectation of what would happen next. One could hear every stringed instrument imaginable, playing together with such harmony that I forgot myself and sat transfixed, to my neighbors' surprise. This lasted nearly half an hour, during which time none of us spoke a word; for as soon as anyone opened his mouth, something invisible gave it a blow without his knowing whence it came. I thought that since we could not see the musicians, I would have liked at least to see all the instruments on which they were playing. After half an hour, this music suddenly ceased, and we saw and heard nothing more.

Soon afterward there arose from outside the door of the hall a great braying and rumbling of trombones, trumpets, and kettledrums, as majestic as if the Roman Emperor himself were making his entrance. Then the door opened by itself, and the brass music grew so loud that we could scarcely bear it. At the same time there came into the hall, as it seemed to me, thousands of little lights, each moving by itself in perfect orderliness, which greatly amazed us. Finally the same two pages entered the hall with bright torches, lighting the way for a beautiful Virgin, riding on a glorious

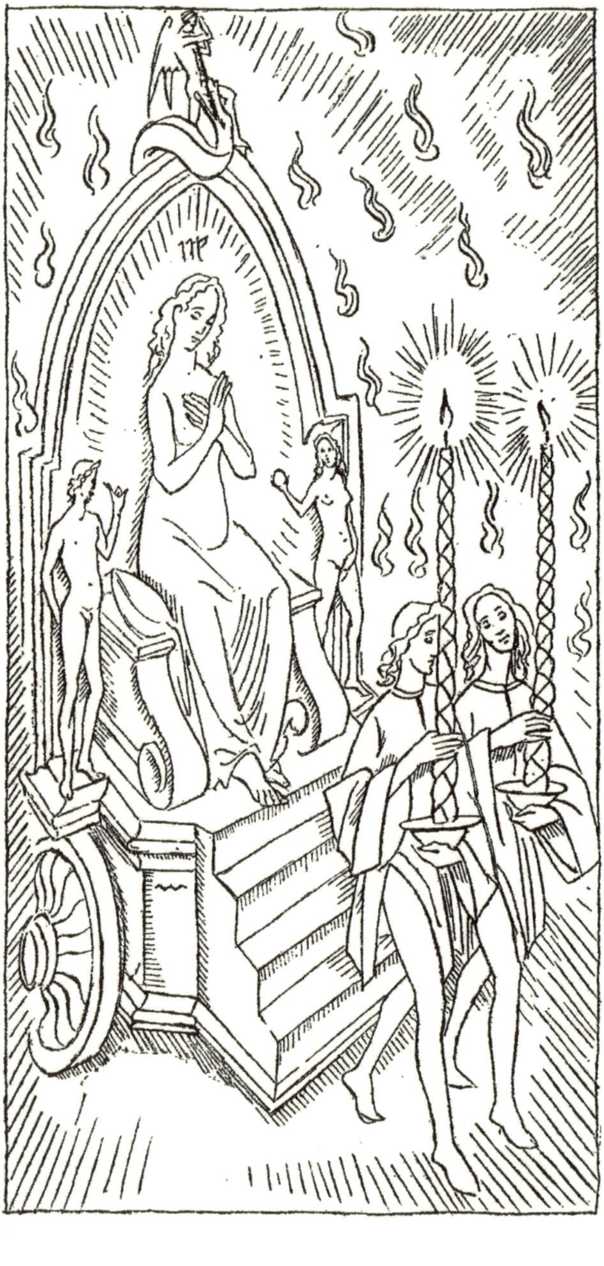

gilded triumphal throne that moved by itself. I thought that she was the same as had formerly lit and extinguished the lights, and that these were her servants whom she had placed by the trees. Now she no longer wore blue, but a shimmering snow-white garment that glittered with pure gold, and she was so bright that we could not keep our eyes on her. The two pages were dressed almost the same, though a little less gorgeously.

As soon as she reached the middle of the hall and stepped down from her seat, all the little lights bowed to her, and we rose from our benches, though each remained standing in his place. After she had shown us, and we her, all honor and reverence, she began to speak with an enchanting voice:

> The King, who is my gracious Lord,
> Is now no longer far away.
> Nor is his best beloved Bride,
> Engaged to be his wedded wife.
> Already now, with great delight,
> They've seen you all arriving here,
> And now, on every one of you
> They would bestow their favor.
> They wish most heartily that you
> May now succeed at every hour
> The coming wedding to enjoy,
> Unmixed with grief for anyone.

Here she bowed courteously again, with all her little lights, and shortly continued:

> The invitation, as you know,
> Said none had been invited here
> Who long before has not received

The proper gifts from God, and who
Is ignorant of how one should
      Behave in such a place.
Therefore let none of you believe
That anyone should be so rash
To go against this hard demand;
You must imagine what it means,
If you have not been long prepared
      This wedding to attend.
Thus they remain in goodly hope
That all things will go well with you.
In these hard times, what joy it is
To see so many gathered here!
But mortals are audacious; their
Unworthiness gives them no pause;
Forward they rudely push themselves
      Where they are not invited.
That no rogue may do business here,
No knave slip in among the rest,
That all of you unhindered may
Enjoy the wedding undefiled,
Tomorrow every one of you
Upon the balance will be weighed.
Whoever is too light reveals
      What he would fain forget.
Whoever in this multitude
Does not possess self-confidence
Will slip off quickly to the side,
For if his welcome he outstays,
All grace and favor he will lose;
Tomorrow he'll be on his way.

> He whose conscience is pricking him
> May stay today within the hall,
> Until tomorrow he is freed;
> > Yet let him not return!
> But he who knows his worthiness,
> His servant will lead out of here
> And show him to his chamber, where
> He may retire and rest, thinking
> The scales will bring him fame,
> > Else will his sleep be hard.
> The others must content themselves,
> For he who dares beyond his powers
> Would have done better not to come.
> > We wish you each the best.

As soon as she had spoken, she made another reverence and jumped gaily back onto her throne. Thereupon the trumpets began to sound again, but many of us could not suppress a deep sigh. The invisibles led her out again, but most of the little lights remained in the hall, one keeping company with each of us.

Our agitation was almost more than I can describe, and fearful thoughts and expressions were exchanged. Most people were still willing to let themselves be weighed, hoping that if they did not succeed, they might be allowed to depart in peace. I myself had thought it over briefly, and, overwhelmed by awareness of my lack of intelligence and unworthiness, I decided to remain in the hall with the others, doing better to content myself with the meal than to court a perilous failure.

After one person here, another there, had been led by his light into a cell (each to an individual one, as I later learned), nine of us remained behind, among whom was the man I had spoken to earlier at table. Our lights did not abandon us, but after an hour one of the pages came in carrying a great bundle of cords, and asked us earnestly if we were determined to stay there. When we assented with a sigh, he bound each of us to a different place, departed with our lights, and left us wretches in the dark.

Then several of us felt the water overflowing its banks, and I myself could not restrain my tears. Although we had not been forbidden to talk to one another, pain and disappointment left us all dumb. The cord was so cunningly made that none could cut it, much less extract our feet. I took scant comfort from the thought that sore disgrace was awaiting many a one now going to his rest, whereas we could pay for our presumption in a single night. At last, in the midst of my heavy thoughts, I fell asleep. For although only a few of us closed our eyes, for sheer exhaustion I could not keep mine open.

As I slept, I had a dream, and though it may not mean much, I do not think it superfluous to tell it. I dreamed I was standing on a high mountain, and saw before me a great wide valley containing an innumerable crowd of people. Each one had a thread attached to his head, by which he was suspended from the sky. Some hung high, others low, while a number were practically standing on the ground. An aged man flew around in the air, holding in his hand a pair of shears with which he here and there snipped off a thread. Whoever hung near to earth landed the sooner, and fell without much noise. But when the turn came for a high one, he would fall so as to shake the ground. It happened to some that their threads were so stretched that they came to earth before they were cut. I much enjoyed the spectacle of this tumbling, and was heartily amused when one who had soared above his station, high in the air, crashed ignominiously and even pulled down some of his neighbors. I was just as glad when one who had kept close to earth all the time was able to land so silently that not even his neighbors noticed.

While my entertainment was at its height, one of my fellow prisoners inadvertently jarred me, so that I awoke and was very annoyed with him. But I thought over my dream and told it to the brother who lay by me on the other side; he was quite amused, and wished that some comfort might be concealed in it. We passed the rest of the night in conversation, and impatiently awaited the coming day.

THE THIRD DAY

As soon as the lovely day had broken and the bright sun had risen over the mountains and begun its appointed task in the high heavens, my good cohorts began to get out of bed and prepare themselves leisurely for the inquisition. One after another came back into the hall, wished us good day, and enquired how we had slept. When they saw our bonds, many of them reproached us for having been so despondent and not, like them, trusted to our luck. There were, however, a few who did not crow so loud, because their hearts were already thumping. We excused ourselves on the grounds of our lack of sense, and hoped that we would get away the quicker unharmed. We bore their mockery with the knowledge that, far from being through with the affair, they perhaps had the worst still to come.

When at length everyone was assembled again, a flourish on the trumpets and drums announced what we could only take to be the imminent arrival of the Bridegroom. But there we were wrong, for it was again the same Virgin as yesterday. She was dressed all in red velvet and girdled with a white ribbon; on her head she wore a green laurel wreath, which suited her splendidly. Her train no longer consisted of little lights, but of nigh on two hundred armed men, all uniformed like her in red and white. As soon as she had leapt from her seat, the Virgin came up to us prisoners, and after greeting us, said shortly:

"That some of you are aware of your wretchedness greatly pleases my severe Lord, and he wishes you to be recompensed." And when she saw me in my habit, she laughed and said:

"Are you also under the yoke? I would have thought that you were too finely turned out!"

With these words my eyes overflowed. Then she gave orders for us to be untied and coupled together, and had us placed so that we could get a good view of the scales. Then she said:

"It may go better for you than for these daredevils who are still free."

Meanwhile the scales, gilded all over, were hung up in the middle of the hall, then a little table was covered with red velvet and seven weights were laid on it. First there was quite a large one, then four small ones, and lastly two more large ones. These weights were so heavy in proportion to their size that no one could believe or even imagine it. Each of the men-at-arms had, beside an unsheathed sword, a strong rope; they were grouped in seven bands corresponding to the number of weights, and in each band one man was assigned to its weight. Then the Virgin leapt back onto her high throne, and as soon as she had made her reverence, she began to speak with a loud voice;

> Whoever enters a painter's shop
> And knows not how to paint,
> And chats of it affectedly,
> > Is a laughing-stock to all.
> Whoever joins a craftsmen's guild
> And has not been elected,
> And plies the craft affectedly,
> > Is a laughing-stock to all.
> Whoever hastens to a wedding
> When no one asked him there,
> Yet enters in affectedly,
> > Is a laughing-stock to all.
> If you should climb upon this scale,
> And find you weigh too light,
> So that you fly up with a crack,
> > You're a laughing-stock to all.

No sooner had the Virgin spoken than she told one of the pages to arrange everyone according to rank and have them mount the scales one after another. One of the Emperors did not hesitate, but bowed slightly to the Virgin and then climbed up in all his state apparel. Each captain laid his weight on, but to everyone's surprise the scale remained unmoved. However, the last weight was too heavy for him, and up he rose, with such disappointment that even the Virgin was sorry for him, it seemed to me. She signaled her people to hold their peace, but the good Emperor was bound and delivered to the sixth band.

After him came a second Emperor, climbing proudly onto the scale, for since he had a great thick book under his robe, he thought he could not fail. Scarcely was the third weight on, when he was shot up into the air so unmercifully that in his terror he let the book fall. This set all the soldiers laughing, and the Emperor was handed over, bound, to the third band. So it went with quite a few emperors, who were all shamefully laughed at and put in captivity.

Next came a short little fellow, also an Emperor, with a curly brown beard. After the customary bow he placed himself on the scale and stood so bravely through the weights that I thought he could even have held out for more, if there had been any. The Virgin quickly arose and went up to him, bowed, and invested him with a red velvet jacket. Then she handed to him one of the many laurel wreaths that lay on her seat, and bade him sit down on the steps below her throne.

It would take too long to tell how it went after this with all the other emperors, kings and lords; but I cannot omit the fact that very few such noble persons were left, although many of them, contrary to my expectation, showed considerable virtues. One could withstand this weight, another that; some two, three, four, or even five; but few were able to attain final perfection. As each one proved too light, the bands of soldiers laughed heartily at him.

The testing proceeded with the noblemen, the scholars, and others, and in each class sometimes one, sometimes two, but more often not a single one was found adequate. Then came the turn of those pious gentlemen the swindlers, and the toadies who manufacture the *Lapidem spitalauficum* [Cure-all stone]. These were put on the scale to such derision that even I, for all my sorrow, almost burst myself laughing, and the prisoners themselves could not suppress their mirth. For most of them could not even wait for the solemn sentence: they were chased from the scales with rods and scourges and led off to join the other prisoners, but each in an appropriate band. So few of the great crowd remained that I would be embarrassed to tell their number; but there were important personages among them, although everyone was honored alike with velvet clothing and a laurel wreath.

When at last the trial was over and no one remained standing off to the side but we poor coupled hounds, one of the captains came up and spoke: "Gracious lady, if it please your grace, we would like to allow these poor people, who have acknowledged their inadequacy, to climb on the scale, too; but without any danger to them, and only in good humor. They may be some worth among them." At first I was greatly afraid, but in my distress was comforted by the thought that in this way I would not have to be held up to derision or whipped out of the scale. I had no doubt that many of the prisoners wished they had spent ten nights with us in the hall. But since the Virgin consented, it had to be done, and so we were untied and one after the other placed on the scale. Although most failed, they were neither mocked nor beaten, but gently ushered to the side. My companion was the fifth; he held out bravely, gratifying many people, especially the captain who had put in a word for us; and the Virgin bestowed on him the customary honor. After him, two more were flipped up in the air.

I was the eighth. As soon as I stepped up, trembling, my companion looked at me encouragingly, sitting there already in his velvet, and even

THE CHEMICAL WEDDING OF CHRISTIAN ROSENKREUZ 95

the Virgin smiled a little. But when I endured through all the weights, she tried to have me tugged up by main force. Yet although three men hung on to the other side of the scales, they could do nothing. Straightway one of the pages stood up and cried out as loud as he could: "It is he!" Whereupon the other answered: "Then let him have his freedom!" And this the Virgin granted.

After I had been inducted with the usual ceremony, I was given the chance of releasing a prisoner of my choice. I did not hesitate for long, but chose the first Emperor, whom I had pitied from the beginning. So he was immediately set free and seated among us with all honor. Now when the last person had been weighed, but the weights proved too heavy for him, the Virgin spied the roses which I had taken from my hat and was holding in my hand. She graciously requested them of me through her page, and I willingly sent them to her. So this first act came to an end about ten o'clock in the morning, and the trumpets were sounded again. However, at the time we still could not see them.

In the meantime, the bands had to go off with their prisoners and await the sentence. Now the five chiefs and ourselves were asked our advice, and the Virgin, as President, gave each one the opportunity to voice his opinion of what should be done with the prisoners. The first suggestion was that they should all be put to death, some more harshly than others, since they had all shamelessly disobeyed the published rules. Others wanted them kept prisoner. But neither suggestion pleased the Virgin, or myself. At last the following proposal was made by the Emperor whom I had released, a nobleman, my companion, and myself: that first, all the distinguished gentlemen should be led out of the castle without delay; then others driven out more ignominiously; yet others thrown out and left to run naked; and a fourth class beaten out with rods or hunted out by hounds. Those who had voluntarily resigned the day before should be let go without any penalty; and finally, the complete rogues and those who had behaved themselves so unseemly at dinner the previous day should be corporally or capitally punished in accordance with their misdeeds.

This proposal pleased the Virgin very much, and was passed. The people were even awarded, as a bonus, a midday meal, and were immediately told of this. But the sentence would also be given at twelve o'clock noon. Here the Senate came to an end, and the Virgin went to her usual quarters with her attendants. We were assigned the highest table in the hall, with the request that we would be content with that until the whole business was finished, after which we would be led to the noble Bridegroom and Bride. To all of which we willingly consented.

Meanwhile, the prisoners were brought back into the hall, and each placed according to his station. They were ordered to behave themselves somewhat better than yesterday, advice which in truth was no longer necessary, since they had completely lost heart. I can honestly state— not that I wish to flatter, but simply as a truth—that in general, the higher-class personages knew better how to conduct themselves in such unexpected misfortune. Their demeanor was poor enough, but honorable; besides, they could not yet see their keepers. But I was very glad to discover that they were now visible to us.

Although fortune had raised us so high, we still did not exalt ourselves over the others, but talked with them and urged them to be of good cheer: it would not turn out so ill. They would have liked to learn their sentences from us, but we were so strictly forbidden to tell them that we let nothing slip. Still, we comforted them as best we could, and drank with them in the hope that the wine might cheer them a little.

Our table was spread with red velvet and laid with pure silver and gold drinking vessels, as the others noticed with astonishment and great chagrin. Before we sat down, the two pages entered and presented us each, in the Bridegroom's name, with the Golden Fleece with a flying lion. We were enjoined to wear this at table, and to guard well the honor and glory of the Order, which His Majesty thus awarded us and would soon confirm with the proper solemnity. This we accepted with the greatest humility, and promised that we would obediently discharge whatever His Majesty should desire. The noble page also had a piece of paper on which we were assigned our places in order. However, I would rather not reveal my place, so as not to be accused of pride, which is against the fourth weight.

Since we had been so magnificently treated, we asked one of the pages whether we were allowed to send some of our food down to our friends and acquaintances; and since no objection was raised, each one sent his friends a generous portion by the servants, who still remained invisible to them. Since they did not know where this was coming from, I decided to take them something myself. Scarcely had I stood up than one of the servants was upon me, saying that he wished he had politely forewarned me: for if one of the pages had seen this, and it had come to the King's ear, it would certainly have turned out badly for me. But since no one had noticed, he was not going to give me away: I, however, should henceforth pay more heed to the honor of my Order. The servant's words really terrified me, so that for a long while I scarcely dared stir in my chair. But I thanked him for his trusty warning, as well as I could in my fear and haste.

Soon the trumpets sounded again. We were quite accustomed to this by now, knowing well that it was the Virgin, so we prepared ourselves to receive her. She entered on her high throne with her usual train, one page bearing before her a tall golden goblet, another a proclamation on parchment. When she had gracefully alighted from her seat, she took the cup from the page and handed it to us in the King's name, with the news that it was sent by His Majesty, to be passed round all of us in his honor. On the lid of this cup stood Fortuna, beautifully crafted of gold, holding in her hand a flying red ensign. For this reason I drank from the cup rather less happily, being all too well acquainted with fortune's tricks.

Our Virgin was now decorated, as we were, with the Golden Fleece and the Lion, from which I observed that she was perhaps the President of the Order. We asked her what the Order's name was, but she answered that it was not time to reveal it, until after the business with the prisoners was over. For this, they were again blindfolded. What had happened to us before now seemed to them mild offence and vexation, and it was as naught in comparison to our present honor. Then she took the proclamation from the second page, divided into two parts, and something like the following was read out to the first group:

"You should confess that you have lent credence too readily to false and spurious books; that you have thought too much of yourselves, and entered this castle to which no one invited you. If perhaps the majority of you simply wanted to slip in here in order to live more grandly and pleasurably, you have egged one another on to such outrage and effrontery that you have well deserved to suffer condign punishment."

They humbly acknowledged it and raised their hands. Then the other group were addressed more harshly in the following terms: "You know very well, and stand convicted by your consciences, that you have forged false and spurious books, fooled and swindled others, thereby lowering the royal dignity in everyone's eyes. You also know what blasphemous and seductive pictures you have used, sparing not even the Holy Trinity, but using it for the cozening of one and all. Now it has come to light what tricks you have played on the rightful guests, and how you have introduced unsuspecting ones. Everyone knows that that you have been involved in open whoring, adultery, debauchery, and every kind of uncleanness, all of it in defiance of the well-known law of our kingdom. In short, you know that you have demeaned His Majesty before the common people; wherefore you should admit that you are publicly convicted swindlers, toadies, and scoundrels, who deserve to be sundered from decent folk and severely punished."

The worthy artists were extremely reluctant to confess to all this. Not only did the Virgin threaten them, on her oath, with death, but the other group shouted loudly against them and complained with one voice that they had been deceitfully seduced by them. In the end, for fear of a still worse fate, they sorrowfully confessed their guilt. But they proposed, in mitigation, that they alone should not be blamed so harshly for what had happened. For when the noblemen were wanting to gain admission to the castle and were laying out great sums of money, each man had used his wits to get some; and so it had come to the present pass, as all could see. Since it had miscarried, in their opinion they deserved no more punishment than the nobles. The latter should surely have had the good judgment to see that one who was certain of getting in would not for mere gain, and in such danger, have clambered over the wall with them. Their books, moreover, had sold so well that anyone who could not live by other means was compelled to practice such a fraud. Therefore they hoped that if justice was to be done, no harm would come to them, since they had behaved as servants should toward their lords, upon the latters' earnest entreaty.

With such arguments they tried to excuse themselves. But they were answered thus: "His Majesty has decided to punish one and all, some more severely, others less so. What you have proposed is indeed partly true, and on that account the nobles will not be entirely acquitted. Those, however, who have acted out of malice or corrupted the ignorant against their will, should prepare to die. Likewise those who have uttered false libels against His Majesty, as all can see from their own writings and books."

Thereupon arose a pitiful weeping and wailing, pleading and prostration, but it was to no avail. I was amazed at how the Virgin stood unmoved by their misery, whereas even we, to many of whom they had caused much suffering and anguish, were moved to pity and tears. Quickly she sent her page, who brought back with him all the men-at-arms who had attended the weighing earlier today. They were then ordered each to take his own band and lead them out in orderly procession to the great garden, every prisoner attended by a cuirassier. It astonished me to see how accurately each soldier recognized his own. My companion of yesterday was also permitted to go freely into the garden and witness the execution of the verdict.

As soon as all were outside, the Virgin leaped from her throne and bade us sit down on the steps and attend the execution. We did as we were told, leaving everything on the table except the goblet, which the Virgin committed to the page's keeping, and, wearing our decorations, mounted the throne. It slid forward by its own power as gently as if it had been floating in the air, and thus we came to the garden where we all dismounted.

This garden was not particularly ornamental, but I was delighted by the way the trees were set out in rank and file. A fine fountain was also running there, decorated with wonderful images and inscriptions, also with strange symbols (which, God willing, I will explain in a future book). A wooden structure was erected in this garden, hung with beautiful painted cloths. It had four galleries, one above the other. The first was the most lordly, hence was hung with a white satin curtain so that we could not tell who was behind. The second was empty and undecorated. The last two were hung with red and blue satin.

As we neared the scaffold, the Virgin bowed almost to the ground, filling us with fear, for we could easily tell that the King and Queen must not be far off. As soon as we too had made obeisance, the Virgin led us by the spiral stair to the second gallery. There she placed herself at the head, and us in the same order as before. For fear of malicious gossip, I cannot now tell how the Emperor whom I had rescued conducted himself toward me, as he had done earlier at table. For he could well see what distress and misery he would now have been in without me, awaiting his sentence in shame, and how, thanks to me, he now stood there in such dignity and honor. Meanwhile, the maiden who had originally brought me the invitation, and whom I had never seen again, stood forth, blew one blast on her trumpet, and with a loud voice pronounced the sentence:

"His Majesty informs all gentlemen present of his sincere wish that one and all assembled here had appeared at his invitation, with such qualities that they might honor him by attending the wedding banquet. But since it has otherwise pleased Almighty God, His Majesty will not complain, but must reluctantly abide by the ancient and laudable usage of this kingdom. However, that His Majesty's innate kindness may be celebrated throughout the world, he has decreed, with his advisors and representatives, that the usual sentence should be considerably mitigated.

"Therefore, in the first place, all noblemen and rulers shall not only have their lives spared, but shall straightway be set free to depart. He asks that your good Lordships be not vexed that you cannot be present at His Majesty's wedding, but reflect that if Almighty God has given you a burden that you cannot easily and patiently bear, he also has an unfathomable wisdom in the distribution of talents. Therefore it shall be no disgrace to your Lordships' reputation to be excluded from such an Order as ours; for we cannot all attain all things.

"Since your Lordships have been misled by evil toadies, these shall not go unpunished. Next, His Majesty wishes to share with you a *Catalogum haereticorum* [Catalogue of heretical writings], or *Index expurgatorium* [Index of things to be purged], whereby you may more wisely sift the good from the bad. And since His Majesty intends before long to overhaul his own library and sacrifice the offending books to Vulcan, he requests your friendship, service, and grace, that each may do likewise with his own, so that hopefully in the future all this evil and rubbish shall be destroyed. Moreover, may you be warned hereby never again to demand admittance here, lest your excuse about seducers be withdrawn and you suffer the contempt and mockery of all. Lastly, since the province has something to demand from your lordships, let none demur to ransom himself with a chain, or whatever he has to hand, and thus depart from us in friendship, and under our escort

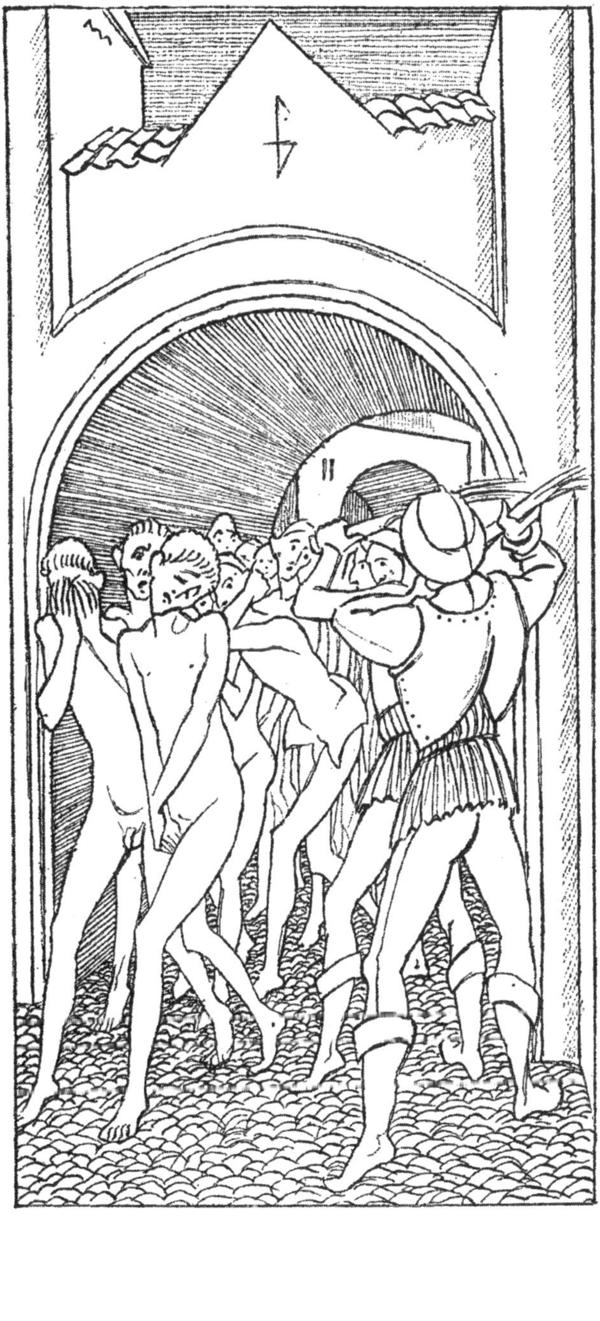

make his way back to his own." The others, however, who did not resist the first, third, and fourth weights, are not so lightly dismissed by His Majesty. That they may also feel his mercy, his command is that they be stripped entirely naked and thus sent away.

"Those who were proved too light by the second and fifth weight shall be stripped and then branded with one, two, or more marks according to how much or little he weighed.

"Those who were raised up only by the sixth or seventh weight shall be treated somewhat more mercifully . . ." (And so forth, a specific punishment being set for each combination, which would take too long to enumerate here.)

"Those who voluntarily resigned yesterday shall be allowed to go free from all obligation.

"Lastly, the arrant swindlers who could not even outweigh a single weight shall suffer capital or corporal punishment according to their deserts, with the sword, the rope, with water, or with rods. And this sentence shall be executed strictly as an example to all." Thereupon our Virgin broke her staff in two. The other maiden, who had read the sentence, sounded her trumpet and with a deep obeisance went to those standing behind the curtain.

I cannot forbear from telling the reader something of the number of our prisoners. Those who equaled one weight were seven; two weights, twenty-one; three weights, thirty-five; four weights, also thirty-five; five weights, twenty-one; six weights, seven. One was raised only with difficulty by all seven weights, and this was the one I had redeemed. Those who failed to raise any weight at all were many; and, lastly, those who raised them all from the ground were few. So I counted them carefully and noted them on my writing tablet, as they stood distinctly before us. It seemed remarkable to me that among all those who weighed anything, no two were exactly the same. For although, as I said, thirty-five of them equaled three weights, in one case it would be the first, second, and third; in another the third, fourth, and fifth; in another, the fifth, sixth, and seventh, and so forth. Thus, amazingly enough, among all the hundred and twenty-six who weighed anything, no two were the same. If time would permit, I would name them all with their respective weights; but I hope it may be published in the future with the interpretation.

Now as this sentence was read out, the nobles were at first quite happy, since in the face of such severity they had not reckoned on getting a light sentence. Thus they gave more than was demanded, each paying with whatever chains, jewelry, gold, money, etc., he had about him, and politely taking his leave. Although the royal servants were forbidden to jeer at them as they went, a few jokers could not keep from giggling; for it was comical enough to see how fast they made their escape without a backward glance. A few asked that the promised catalogue might be sent them at once, for they wanted to deal with their books as would please His Majesty. This was also promised them. Beneath the porch each was given a beaker of *Oblivionis haustus* [Draught of forgetfulness], so that he might forget his misfortune.

After these, the volunteers departed; they were allowed to go because of their good sense, but never again might they return in the same condition. However, if they, like the others, should receive further revelations, they would be welcome guests.

Meanwhile the culprits were being stripped, and here too appropriate distinctions were made. Some were driven away naked but unmolested; some were decked out with bells and jingles; some pursued with whips. In short, the penalties were so various that I cannot enumerate them all. Finally it came to the last ones, whose treatment lasted a little longer; for it took a considerable time for some to be hanged, some beheaded or drowned, and others put to death in different ways. My eyes truly ran over at this execution, not so much because of the punishments, which they had well deserved for their crimes, but in reflection on human

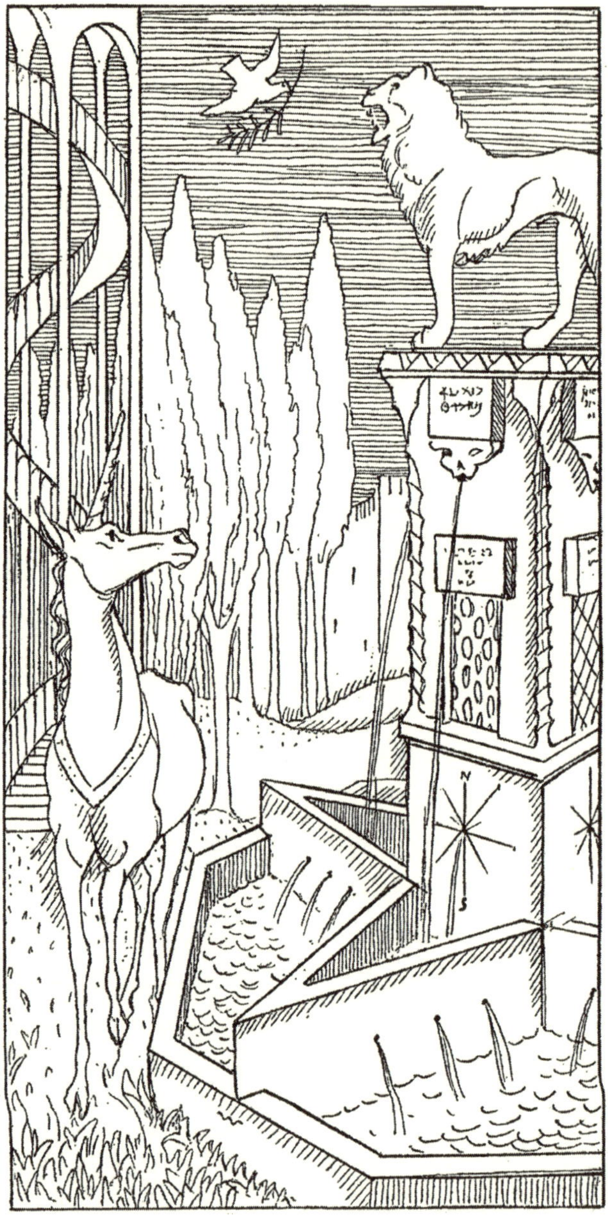

delusion, in that we are always meddling in that which has been sealed up for us since the Fall of Man.

Now the garden, formerly so crowded with people, was almost empty, and none but the men-at-arms remained. When all was over, there was silence for five minutes. Then there came a beautiful, snow-white unicorn with a golden collar on which were certain letters; it stepped up to the fountain and knelt down on its forelegs, as if it wished to honor the lion which stood upon the fountain, so still that I had taken it for stone or bronze. Immediately the lion took the naked sword that it held in its claws, and broke it in two in the middle, whereupon the pieces appeared to me to sink in the water. Then it roared long, until a white dove flew up, bringing in its little beak a sprig of olive, which the lion straightway swallowed and was satisfied. The unicorn also returned contentedly to its place.

Hereupon our Virgin led us down the spiral stair from the wooden structure, and we again made our obeisance toward the curtain. Then we had to wash our hands and heads in the fountain, and wait a little while in our order until the King had returned to his hall through a concealed passageway. We were conducted out of the garden and back to our former quarters with special music, in great pomp and splendor, and with elevated conversation. This was toward four o'clock in the afternoon.

In order to make the time pass more quickly, the Virgin had appointed each of us a well-bred page, not only richly dressed but also well educated. These pages could discourse on any subject so knowingly that we were quite put to shame. They had the duty of showing us around the castle, though not everywhere, so as to pass the time and satisfy our curiosity. Meanwhile the Virgin took her leave, promising us that she would reappear at supper and then celebrate the ceremony of *suspensionis ponderum* [hanging of the weights]. She bade us await the next day with patience, for then we must be presented to the King.

When she had taken leave of us, each one did as he pleased. Some looked at the beautiful pictures that were shown to them, and were curious to know what the mysterious symbols might mean. Others needed to refresh themselves again with food and drink. But I let myself be guided round the palace by my page, together with my companion, and will never regret that tour as long as I live; for among many wonderful antiquities I was also shown the Tombs of the Kings, where I learned more than is to be found in all the books in the world. There, too, stands the miraculous Phoenix, about which I published a special booklet two years ago. (I also intend, if my narrative should prove fruitful, to publish separate treatises on Lions, Eagles, Gryphons, Falcons, and other things, with their illustrations and inscriptions.) I am only sorry that my other companions missed such treasures; yet I suppose this must have been God's express desire. I was especially glad of my page, for according to each person's interest, his page led him into the places and situations that he would enjoy. Mine alone was entrusted with the keys to this place, because this pleasure was reserved especially for me. Others, indeed, were invited, but they thought that such tombs would only be found in the churchyard, to which they would come soon enough if there were anything worth seeing there. But I would not withhold from my grateful students the tombs that the two of us drew and transcribed.

The other thing shown to us both was the marvelous library. Everything was there, complete, as before the Reformation. But even though my heart leaps whenever I think of it, I will not yet tell about it, because its catalogue is shortly to be published. By the entrance to this room stood an enormous book such as I had never seen, in which were pictured all the figures, chambers, portals, all the inscriptions, riddles, and suchlike, to be seen in the whole castle. Although I have also promised to give some of these, it seems not yet the proper time; I must first learn to know the world better. In every book the author's portrait was painted. Many of these, as I understood, were to be burnt, so that their memory would be blotted out among righteous men.

THE CHEMICAL WEDDING OF CHRISTIAN ROSENKREUZ

When we had perused these things and had just left, another page ran up to us and whispered something into our page's ear. The latter gave up the keys to him, which the other immediately took up the spiral staircase. Our page had turned as white as death, and when we beset him with questions, he informed us that His Majesty wanted no one to visit either the Library or the Tombs; hence he begged us, for his life's sake, not to give him away to anyone, since he had just denied it. This we also promised him, half in joy and half in fear, and fortunately it remained secret, for no one asked us any more about it. We had spent three hours in the two places, which I will never regret.

Although it had already struck seven, we had still been given nothing to eat; but our hunger was easily satisfied by the continual stimulation, and I could have fasted my life long on nourishment like this. We were also shown ingenious waterworks, mines, and various ateliers, none of which failed to surpass all of our arts and crafts taken together. The rooms were all arranged in a semicircle, so that they had a view of the splendid mechanical clock mounted on a beautiful tower in the center, and could regulate themselves according to the movements of the planets, which were charmingly depicted on it. There again it was clear to me how far short our own artists fall, although it is not my business to instruct them.

At length we came to a large hall, which the others had been shown long before. In the middle stood a terrestrial globe thirty feet in diameter, although nearly half of it, except a little that was covered by the steps, was sunk in the ground. Two men could easily turn this globe and its apparatus, so that the same amount was always visible above the horizon. Although I could well see that this instrument had some particular purpose, I could not understand what was served by the small golden circles visible at various places on it. My page laughed at this and told me to examine them more closely. I found thereon my own country, also marked with gold, whereupon my companion searched for his own and found it likewise. Since this was also the case with the other bystanders, the page assured us that yesterday the old astronomer Atlas had shown His Majesty that the gilded points indicated with perfect accuracy the homes of all the elect. For this reason the page, too, when he saw that I had excluded myself, although there was a mark on my country, had instructed one of the captains to plead for us, that we might take our chances on the scales without risk, especially since the country of one of us had a remarkably favorable sign. Hence also he, who of all the pages had the most influence, had not been assigned to me without reason. I thanked him for this and looked more carefully at my native land, noticing that near the circle were some delicate rays (though I do not mention this for my own name and fame). I saw much more on this globe that I prefer not to reveal; everyone may ask himself why every town does not have its philosopher.

After this he led us right into the globe. It was made so that in the ocean, where there was otherwise a great empty space, there was a tablet with three dedications and the artist's name. One could raise this gently, and gain access via a slender bridge to the center, where there was room for four people. Nothing else was inside but a round bench on which we sat, and even in full daylight (it was now dark) could contemplate the stars. I think these were made from pure carbuncles, glittering so beautifully in their proper order and courses that I could scarcely bear to leave, as the page later told our Virgin, for which she often teased me. For it was already mealtime, and I had stared so long inside the globe that I was almost the last at table.

I could tarry no longer, and as soon as I had put on my gown, which I had laid aside, I came to the table. The servants greeted me with such bowing and scraping that I dared not look up for shame, and thus accidentally left the Virgin standing as she awaited me to one side. As soon as she noticed, she pulled me by the gown and led me to table. I need tell no more about the music and other delights, partly because I am quite unworthy to describe them, and partly because I have already done so as best I can. In a word, there was nothing but artistry and beauty. After we had told each other of our various experiences of the afternoon (though the Library and the Tombs were not mentioned), and were feeling merry from the wine, the Virgin began to speak:

"Gentlemen, I am having a great argument with one of my sisters. In our room we have an eagle which we are both feeding diligently in order to win his affection, and this has caused much ill-will. One day we decided to go to him together, and let him belong to whichever of us he was most friendly to. We did so, with myself, as usual, carrying a branch of laurel in my hand. When the eagle saw us both, he quickly gave my sister a twig that he had in his beak, and then begged for mine, which I gave him. Now each one believes that he likes her the best. What should I do about this?"

We all enjoyed the Virgin's modest proposal, and everyone would gladly have heard the solution; but since all their eyes rested on me, and they wanted me to begin, I was so muddled in my head that I could do nothing but ask another riddle. So I said: "Gracious Lady, it would be easy to answer your question if it were not for a trouble of my own. I had two friends, both extraordinarily attached to me. Since they could not decide which of them loved me the most, they made up their minds to run up to me unawares. Whoever I embraced first, he would be the one. This they did, but since one could not keep up with the other, he was left behind and wept. I received the other with surprise. When they explained the trick, I knew no way out, and so I have been stuck to this day, in the hope of finding good counsel here."

The Virgin thought this over, well seeing what I was about, and therefore answered: "Very good, then let us two be quits! Let the others propose a solution!"

But I had already made them wise, and so a second one began: "In my town a maiden was lately condemned to death. But the judge was so sorry that he let it be known that if anyone would fight for her, she should be his. Now she had two lovers. One immediately came to the lists to await his adversary. Then the other also presented himself, but since he came too late, he decided all the same to fight for her, and willingly let himself be beaten, so that her life would be spared. And this he did. Afterward both of them wanted her. Now tell me, gentlemen, which of the two had won her?"

Then the Virgin could hold back no longer, and said: "I hoped to learn much, but now I am ensnared myself. Still, I would like to hear if anyone else has something to say."

"Indeed," answered a third, "never has a stranger story been told than what once happened to me. In my youth I was in love with a virtuous girl. In order to bring my love to its desired goal, I employed an old woman who would take me with her to visit the girl. Now it happened that the girl's brothers came upon us while the three of us were alone together. They were so angry that they wanted to kill me, but I implored them so much that they finally made me swear to take each one to wife for a year. Now tell me, gentlemen: should I have taken the older or the younger one first?" We all laughed heartily at this riddle, and although some whispered together, none wanted to make the choice.

Then a fourth began: "There lived in a town an honorable, aristocrat's wife whom many admired, but especially a young nobleman. He became so importunate that she finally gave him this ultimatum: he could have his way if, in the middle of winter, he could lead her into a beautiful green rose garden; if not, then he could never see her again. Thereupon the nobleman traveled in every land to find a man who could bring this about, until at last he came upon an old fellow who promised to do it on condition that he would give him the half of his possessions. He agreed, and the other arranged it. He invited the woman to his garden, and to her astonishment she found everything green, pleasant, and warm. When she remembered her vow, she asked to go once more to her husband, to whom she poured out her sorrow with sighs and tears. He, however, knowing well her faithfulness, sent her back to her lover who had bought her so dear, to redeem her promise. The nobleman was so moved by the husband's integrity that he felt it would be sinful to touch so virtuous a wife, and sent her back honorably to her husband. Now, when the little old man learnt of their fidelity, poor as he was, he did not want to be left out; so he gave the nobleman back all his property, and departed. Now, gentlemen, I do not know which of these people displayed the greatest virtue."

This tale left us all speechless; even the Virgin had no answer but to ask another of us to go on. So the fifth began without delay: "Gentlemen, I will make it short. Who has the greater joy: the one who beholds his beloved, or the one who only has her in his thoughts?" "The one who sees her," said the Virgin. "No," I replied, whereupon an argument began. Then the sixth cried out: "Gentlemen, I would take a wife; but I have the choice of a maiden, a married woman, and a widow. Help me out of my dilemma, and I will help you settle yours."

"Nothing easier," replied the seventh, "if you have the choice. But for me things are different. In my youth I loved a beautiful, virtuous girl from the bottom of my heart, and she loved me, but her kinsman would not give permission for us to marry. So she was married to another man, honest and upright, who kept her with modesty and affection until she came to childbed, and was so ill that everyone thought she had died. With great sorrow, they gave her a magnificent burial. Then I thought to myself: if this person could not be yours in life, at least you can embrace her in death and kiss her to your heart's content. So I took my servant with me, and dug her up again by night. When I opened the coffin and took her in my arms, I felt her heart and discovered that it was still beating a little. As I warmed her it became stronger and stronger, until I could see that she was indeed still alive. Then I silently took her home with me and, after warming her frozen body with a bath of precious herbs, entrusted her to my mother until she gave birth to a fine son. I had both of them given the utmost care.

After two days, since she was greatly confused, I revealed to her all that had occurred, and asked her to live as my wife from now on. But she was greatly worried that it might give grief to her husband, who had treated her well and honorably. Be that as it may, she now felt no less obligated by love of one as of the other.

"After two months, being obliged to travel elsewhere, I invited her husband as a guest and asked him among other things whether he would take back his dead wife, if she were to come home again. He affirmed it with tears and lamentations. Finally I brought his wife to him, together with her son, told him all that had happened, and asked him to give consent for my intended marriage. After a long argument he could not shake my claim, and so had to leave the wife with me. Then came the battle over the son..."

The Virgin here interrupted him and said: "I am surprised that you could thus increase the poor man's misery."

"What?" he answered. "Was I not concerned about it?"

Thereupon an argument arose among us, in which most of us were of the opinion that he had done right. But he said: "Not at all: I gave him back both wife and son! Now tell me, gentlemen, which was the greater: my integrity or this man's happiness?"

These words had so aroused the Virgin that she straightway had a toast sent round in honor of these two. Then followed the stories of the others; but since they were somewhat confused, I cannot recall them all. Only one still occurs to me. He said that a few years ago he knew a physician who had bought wood against the winter, and the whole winter long had kept himself warm with it. But when spring approached, he sold the same wood again and thus warmed himself for nothing. "That must be an art!" said the Virgin, "But it is too late for it today." "Yes," answered my companion, "whoever cannot solve all the riddles should ask for the answers by messenger. This, I think, cannot be refused."

Now grace was said, and we all stood up from the table, more satisfied and merry than glutted; I could wish that all feasts and meals were conducted thus. As we were taking a turn or two in the hall, the Virgin asked us whether we would like to make a start with the wedding. "Gladly," said one, "O noble and virtuous maiden!"

Thereupon she discreetly sent a page off, but continued in conversation with us. She was so familiar with us that I was bold enough to ask her name. Then the Virgin smiled at my impertinence, but did not get annoyed, and answered instead:

"My name contains five-and-fifty, and has but eight letters. The third is the third part of the fifth; if it is added to the sixth, they make a number whose root exceeds the first letter by as much as the third itself, and is half of the fourth. The fifth and seventh are equal, and the last is equal to the first, and these make as much with the second as the sixth, which is just four more than thrice the third. Now tell me, Sir, what is my name?"

The riddle seemed thorny enough. However, I did not give up, but asked: "Noble and virtuous maiden, might I not know a single letter?" "Yes," she said, "that would be all right." "Then how much," I went on, "would the seventh be worth?" "It is as many as the gentlemen here." Then I was satisfied, and easily worked out her name.[3] This pleased her, and she said that more would be revealed to us soon.

In the meantime, a number of maidens had made themselves ready and now entered with great show. Before them two youths lighted the way; one had a cheerful face, bright eyes, and a fine figure, but the other looked somewhat petulant—whatever he wanted, must be done, as I afterward learnt. Next followed four maidens: one of them very demure in her conduct, looking modestly at the ground; the second equally modest and bashful; the third was frightened of something as she entered the room. As I understood it, she cannot long remain where people are too hearty. The fourth carried some bouquets to indicate her friendliness and generosity.

---

3 The Virgin's name is ALCHIMIA.

THE CHEMICAL WEDDING OF CHRISTIAN ROSENKREUZ

After these four maidens came two others, more elaborately dressed, and greeted us courteously. One wore a deep blue dress set with little golden stars; the other was all in green, ornamented with red and white stripes. Both had loose kerchiefs on their heads, which looked utterly charming. Lastly came one on her own who wore a coronet on her head, and looked up to heaven rather than to earth. We all thought she must be the Bride, but were far wrong, although she so outdid the Bride in nobility, wealth, and status that she afterward dominated the whole wedding feast.

At this point we all followed the example of our Virgin, sinking deep on our knees, although the lady behaved very humbly and reverently. She offered each her hand, and bade us not to be too surprised at this, for it was the least of her gifts. But we should lift our eyes to our Creator and learn to recognize his omnipotence here, then lead our lives as before, using this grace for the glory of God and the good of mankind. Her words were very different from those of our Virgin, who was somewhat more worldly; they pierced through my very marrow. "And you," she went on, addressing me, "have received more than others; see that you also give more!" This sermon puzzled me greatly.

When we noticed the maidens with instruments, we thought we were going to have to dance, but the time had not yet come. The weights, about which I have told, were still all there. Hence the Queen (though I still did not know who she was) told each maiden to take one of them. She gave her own, the last and biggest, to our Virgin and bade us follow her. Now our prestige was somewhat lessened, and I was well aware that our Virgin had been too kind to us, and that we were not valued as highly as we had sometimes begun to imagine. So we went out in our usual order until we reached the first room, where our Virgin was the first to hang up the Queen's weight. Then a beautiful anthem was sung.

In this room was nothing valuable but some fine little prayer books, such as one should never be without. In the middle stood a tall lectern, excellently suited for prayer. The Queen knelt down at this, and we all had to kneel around her and pray after her as she read from one of the books, namely that the wedding might go forward to God's glory and to our benefit. Then we moved to the second room, where the first maiden hung up her weight, and so forth until the ceremony was completed. Thereupon the Queen again gave each her hand and took her leave with her maidens.

Our President stayed with us a while, but since it was already two o'clock in the morning, she did not want to keep us longer. It was my impression that she enjoyed being with us. She wished us a good night and a peaceful sleep, but it seemed as if she parted from us unwillingly. Our pages knew their business well; they showed each to his bedroom and remained with us in another bed, so as to be at hand if we should need anything. My bedroom (I know nothing of the others) was royally furnished and hung with beautiful tapestries and paintings. Most of all I liked my page; he was so well informed and accomplished that he kept me up for yet another hour, and I did not fall asleep until half past three.

That was the first night I went to sleep in peace. Nevertheless, a dreadful dream kept me from being too contented: all night long I was struggling with a door I could not open. Finally I succeeded, and in such fantasies passed the time until, toward dawn, I awoke.

THE FOURTH DAY

I WAS STILL lying in my bed, calmly looking at the wonderful pictures and sculptures that filled my room, when suddenly I heard cornetts playing, as if the procession had already started. My page jumped out of bed like a mad thing, looking more dead than alive; and you can imagine how I felt, too, when he said that the others were already being presented to the King. I did not know what to do, beyond weeping bitterly and bemoaning my laziness, but I got dressed. My page was ready much sooner and ran out of the room to see how things stood. Soon he returned, bringing the welcome news that nothing was lost: I had merely slept through breakfast, and they had not had me woken on account of my age. But now it was time to go with him to the fountain, where most of them were assembled.

My spirits rose on hearing this, and I was soon ready in my outfit. I followed the page to the fountain in the same garden as yesterday. When we had greeted one another, and the Virgin had teased me for a slug-a-bed, she led me by the hand to the fountain. Here I found that the lion, instead of his sword, had a largish tablet, which on closer examination I found to be taken from the ancient monuments and put here in the place of honor. The writing had deteriorated from age, but all the same I will give it here for anyone to meditate on:

HERMES PRINCEPS.
POST TOT ILLATA
GENERI HUMANO DAMNA,
DEI CONSILIO:
ARTISQUE ADMINICULO,
MEDICINA SALUBRIS FACTUS
HEIC FLUO.
Bibat ex me qui potest: lavet, qui vult :
turbet qui audet:
BIBITE FRATRES ET VIVITE.

[Prince Hermes. After so many injuries done to the human race, by God's counsel, and by the aid of art, here I flow, made a healing medicine. Drink from me who can; wash who wishes; stir who dares; drink, brethren, and live.]

This writing was simple to read and understand, so it can well be given here, being easier than the rest. After we had begun by washing in the fountain, each took a drink from a solid gold beaker. Then we had to follow the Virgin once more into the hall, and there don new clothes of cloth of gold, beautifully decorated with flowers. Each one was given a second Golden Fleece, set with precious stones and each worked according to the individual craftsman's skill. On it hung a heavy piece of gold picturing the sun and moon opposite one another. On the reverse was this saying: "The moon's light shall be like the sun's light, and the sun's light shall be seven times as bright as now." Our previous decorations were put in a case and entrusted to one of the servants.

After this the Virgin led us in order outside, where the musicians were already waiting by the door, all dressed in red velvet with white borders. Thereupon a door, which I had never seen open before, was opened to the royal staircase. The Virgin led us and the musicians up its 365 spiral steps. Here we saw nothing but fine and precious workmanship; the higher we went, the more splendid the decorations became. At length we came out at the top into a painted vault, where sixty maidens were awaiting us, all daintily dressed. They bowed to us, and we made our reverence to them as best we could, then our musicians were sent back down the stairs and the door was shut. A little bell was rung, whereupon a beautiful maiden entered, bringing each one a laurel wreath, while our maidens were given branches.

Then a curtain was drawn back, and I saw the King and Queen sitting there in their majesty. And if yesterday's Queen had not been so kind as to warn me, I would have forgotten myself and compared such unspeakable splendor to Heaven itself; for though the room shone with pure gold and precious stones, the Queen's robes were such that I could not look on them. It was all as far above what I had formerly thought beautiful as the stars in the sky. Now the Virgin came in, and taking each of the maidens by the hand presented her with a deep bow to the King.

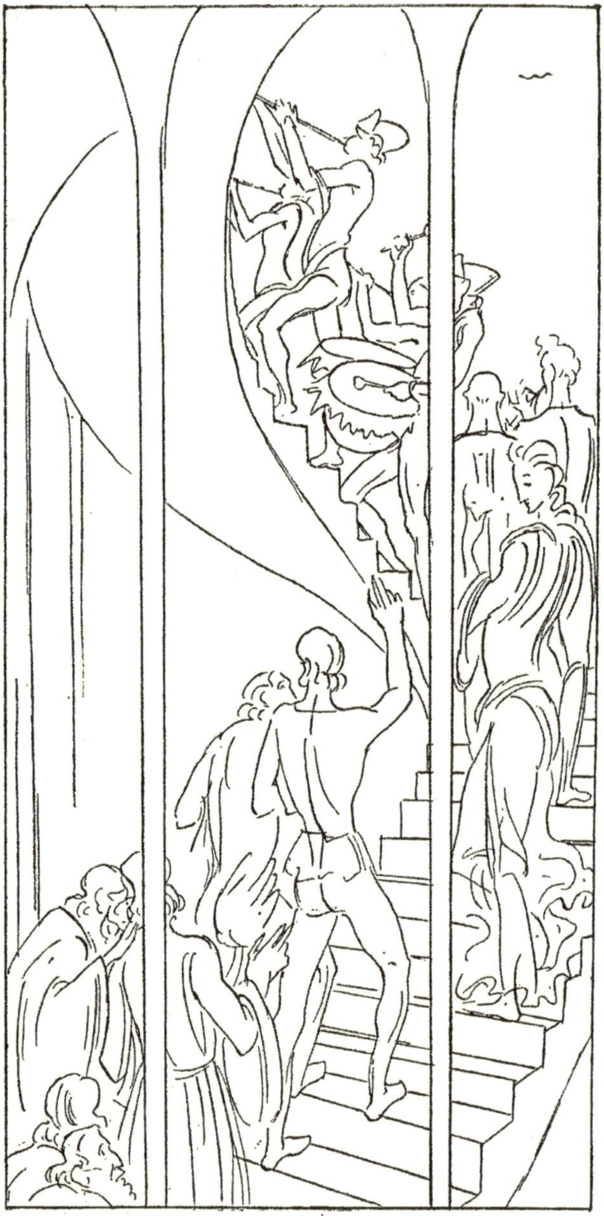

Then the Virgin spoke: "May it please Your Majesties, gracious King and Queen: the gentlemen here present have come at the risk of life and limb. Your Majesties have reason to rejoice, since the majority are well qualified to contribute to Your Majesties' kingdom and estates, as will be ascertained from each one. I therefore pray to present them humbly to Your Majesties, and humbly beg to be discharged of this my commission, and that each be questioned graciously about my deeds and omissions."

Thereupon she laid her branch on the ground. It would have been fitting now if one of us had said a few words, but we were all tongue-tied. At last the aged Atlas came and spoke on the King's behalf: "Their Majesties are well pleased by your arrival, and wish one and all to receive their royal favor. They are well satisfied with your conduct, dear maiden, on which account a royal honor will be reserved for you. But they think that you should continue to attend them today, as they have nothing with which to reproach you." The Virgin therefore took up her branch again, and for the first time we had to withdraw with our own maidens.

The front of this chamber was rectangular, five times as long as it was broad. Toward the exit it had a great arch like a portal in which stood in a circle three splendid royal thrones, the middle one somewhat higher than the others. Two people sat on each throne. On the first was an old king with a gray beard, but his consort was very beautiful and young. On the third throne sat a black king of middle age, and beside him a dainty old matron, not crowned but wearing a veil. On the middle throne sat the two young persons with laurel wreaths on their heads, while over them hung a great ornamental crown. They were not as attractive as I had imagined them, but so it must be. Behind them on a curved bench sat a number of old men, none of whom, to my surprise, wore a sword or any other weapon; I also saw no bodyguards. Some of the maidens who had been with us yesterday were sitting along the side of the arch.

Here I must mention something else. Little Cupid flew around, especially flitting playfully about the great crown. Sometimes he sat

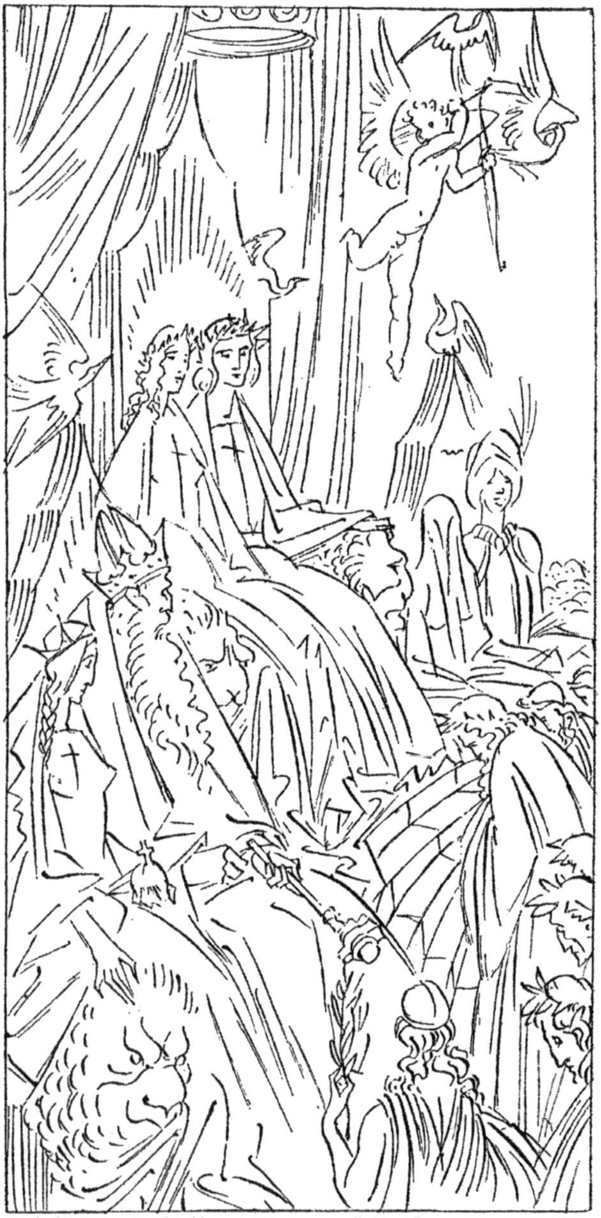

between the lovers and teased them with his bow, and now and then he even seemed about to shoot one of us. In short, the child was so mischievous that he would not even leave the little birds alone that flew in great numbers around the chamber, but annoyed them whenever he could. The maidens had a short way with him, and when they caught him he could not easily escape. This little knave provided great diversion and amusement.

Before the Queen stood an altar, small but exquisitely decorated, on which were a black velvet book discreetly overlaid with gold, and beside it a small taper in an ivory candlestick. For all its smallness it burned on and on unmoving, and if Cupid had not sometimes blown on it for fun, we would not have taken it for a fire. Near this stood a sphere or celestial globe, turning neatly on its own; also a little striking clock; and next a tiny crystal fountain out of which a clear blood-red liquid continually ran; and lastly a skull in which was a white snake, so long that although it crawled round and encircled all the objects, its tail remained in one of the eyeholes of the skull until its head came back to the other, so that it never left its skull. But if Cupid tweaked it a little, it instantly vanished inside, leaving us all astounded.

Besides this altar, here and there in the chamber were wonderful images which moved as if they were alive, and were full of such fantasy that I cannot possibly describe them all. As we left the room, there arose an extraordinary music of voices; I could not say whether it came from the maidens who were still inside, or from the images themselves.

Being now well satisfied, we exited with our maidens and found our musicians all ready to conduct us down the spiral staircase; but the door was carefully locked and bolted. As soon as we were back in the hall, one of the maidens began: "Sister, I was surprised that you dared go among so many people." "My sister," answered our President, "None of them worried me so much as this one!" and she pointed to me. This speech hurt my feelings, for I could well see that she was mocking my old age. And indeed, I was the oldest of all. Then she comforted me again with the assurance that if I would behave myself with her, she would certainly relieve me of this burden.

Now the meal was brought in and each sat beside his maiden. They well knew how to make the time fly with charming conversation, but I must not chatter about their gossip and games out of school. Most of the talk was about the arts, by which I learnt soon enough that young and old were well acquainted with them. But I was still thinking about how I might make myself young again, and this made me sad.

The Virgin, seeing this, said: "I know what this young fellow needs: if I were to sleep with him the coming night, he would be happier in the morning." Then they started to laugh, and although I blushed from head to toe, I had to laugh at my own misfortune. There was one who tried to turn my shame back on the Virgin, saying: "I hope that not only we but the maidens themselves will bear witness to our brother that our Virgin President has promised to sleep with him tonight." "I should be happy at that," answered the Virgin, "if I had not my own sisters here to fear; for what would they do if I were to choose the fairest and best without their leave?" "My sister," began another, "we can see from this that your high office has not made you proud. If by your permission we may make these gentlemen our bedfellows, choosing them by lot, we are most happy for you to exercise your prerogative."

We left it at that, thinking it a joke, and began to talk to each other, but our Virgin would not leave us in peace, and began again: "Sirs, what if we let chance decide who should sleep with whom tonight?" "Very well," I said, "if it must be, we cannot refuse such an offer." It was decided to try it after the meal, and since we did not want to stay longer at table we stood up, and each walked up and down with his maiden. "No," said the Virgin, "this must not be: we will see how chance pairs us," whereupon we were separated again.

Now a dispute arose about how this should be done, but this was a premeditated plan, for the Virgin soon made the suggestion that we should mingle with one another in a ring; she would begin to count from herself, and every seventh one must take the next seventh for lover, be it man or maid. Since we saw no trick in it, we let it go ahead, thinking that we were well mixed up; but the maidens were so crafty that each one already knew her position. The Virgin began to count, and the seventh was another maiden; the next seventh, a maiden again, and so forth, to our astonishment, until every maiden was out, and none of us were hit upon! We poor souls were left standing all alone to suffer merciless teasing, and admit that we had been thoroughly foxed. If anyone had seen us in our ring, he would have thought it more likely for the heavens to fall than for the counting never to come to us. With this our games came to an end, and we had to be reconciled with the Virgin's practical joke.

Now wanton little Cupid came in again, but as a messenger from Their Majesties, who thereby sent us a drink in a golden beaker. He also summoned our maidens to attend the King, explaining that he could not tarry with them now, nor could we make sport with him. We let him fly off with the appropriate message of our humble thanks. Since in the meantime my companions' spirits had sunk to their feet, which the maidens were not sorry to see, they started up a gentle dance, which I preferred to watch rather than join. My mercurial friends, however, went to work on it as skillfully as if they had long learnt their trade. After a few dances, our President returned and told us that the artists and students had petitioned to honor and entertain Their Majesties before their departure by acting a pleasant comedy; and that if it was our desire to attend, we might accompany Their Majesties to the House of the Sun; that they would be pleased and would receive us graciously there. We first thanked them with the deepest humility for this honor, then prayed them to accept our unworthy service.

The Virgin took this message and returned with the command to await Their Majesties in our usual order in the gallery. We were led thither, and did not wait long, for the royal procession was already at hand, yet without any music. In front went the unknown Queen who had been with us yesterday, clothed in white satin with an elegant coronet; otherwise she carried nothing but a small crucifix made from a single pearl, which had been revealed today between the young King and his Bride. After her came the same six maidens as before, in two groups, carrying the King's regalia belonging to the little altar. Next came the three Kings with the Bridegroom in the middle, but he was quite plainly dressed, just in black satin, Italian style, and wearing a small round hat with a little black pointed feather. He doffed it to us courteously, to show his favor toward us, while we bowed (as we had to the previous one) as we had been instructed. After the Kings came the three Queens, of whom two were richly dressed. The one in the middle was also all in black, and Cupid carried her train. Here we were signaled to follow, and after us the maidens, until old Atlas brought up the rear.

In such procession we came at last through many an elegant walk to the House of the Sun, where we took our places near the King and Queen on a specially erected platform, to watch the comedy that had been prepared. We were on the right of the Kings, though separated from them, and the maidens on their left, except those in charge of the royal insignia, who were given a special place at the top. Any other servants had to stand below, between the pillars, and make the best of it.

Now since much in this comedy was strange and remarkable, I must not fail to give a brief summary of it.

[Act One] To begin with, an old King came out with several servants. A small chest was brought to his throne, with the news that it had been found on the water. When it was opened, there was a lovely baby, a few jewels, and a small letter on parchment, sealed and addressed to the King. He opened it immediately, but after he had read it broke into tears and informed his servants that the Moorish King had done him a great injury, seizing the lands of his kinswoman and murdering the entire royal lineage, right down to this infant. (He had previously intended to marry her daughter to his own son.) The King swore eternal enmity toward the Moor and his accomplices, and to wreak revenge. Then he ordered the baby to be nursed tenderly, and himself to be armed against the Moor. This preparation, and the girl's upbringing (for after she was a little older, she was put under an old tutor) lasted the whole first act, with many a fine and excellent diversion.

[First Interlude] Here a lion was set to fight a gryphon, and the lion won, which was very good to watch.

[Act Two] In the second act, the Moor came on, a spiteful black man. He had learnt to his fury that his massacre had been discovered, but that a little girl had been rescued from him by stealth. He wondered how he could counter so powerful an enemy by treachery, and was advised by some who had fled to him to escape famine. Against everyone's expectations, the girl fell into his clutches again, and he would certainly have had her strangled if he had not been cleverly deceived by his own servants. This act closed with a splendid triumph of the Moor.

[Act Three] In the third act, a great army was assembled by the King against the Moor, commanded by a brave old knight, who invaded the Moor's land and at last rescued the girl from the tower and clothed her again. After this they quickly raised a splendid platform and placed their young lady upon it. Soon came twelve royal messengers, among whom the same elderly knight made a speech, saying that his most gracious King had not only saved her from death before now, but had her raised in regal fashion, though she had not always behaved properly. Now he had chosen her before all others as wife to the young lord his son, and wished this wedding to take place without delay, so long as she would swear to him the following articles. Here he had read out from a parchment certain admirable conditions, which would be well worth recounting if it would not take too long. In brief, the maiden swore an oath to keep them faithfully, and thanked him most gracefully for this high favor. Then they all set to singing the praises of God, the King, and the maiden, and thus exited for the time being.

[Second Interlude] As a diversion, the four beasts of Daniel were brought on, as he saw them in his vision and minutely described them, all of which had a certain significance.

[Act Four] In the fourth act, the maiden was restored to her lost kingdom and crowned, and for a while was joyfully paraded in the courtyard with all ceremony. Many ambassadors presented themselves, not only to wish her well, but also to admire her finery. But her good conduct did not last for long: soon she was looking around herself saucily and winking at the ambassadors and other lords, in which she thoroughly acted out the role. Her behavior soon came to the ears of the Moor, who did not want to let such an opportunity slip. Since her steward did not keep proper guard over her, she was easily seduced with extravagant promises, so that she lost her confidence in the King and secretly fell by degrees under the Moor's influence. Thereupon he made haste, and when he had brought her willingly into his power he charmed her with words until her whole kingdom became subject to him. Then, in the third scene of this act, he had her led out and stripped entirely naked, bound to a pillar on a rough wooden scaffold, well whipped, and finally condemned to death. This was so pitiful to see that many eyes ran over. Then she was thrust naked into the dungeon to await her death, which was to be by poison. It did not kill her, however, but left her completely leprous. So this act was largely tragic.

[Third Interlude] In between they brought out Nebuchadnezzar's image, decorated with many coats of arms on its head, breast, belly, thighs, feet, etc., which will also be discussed in the forthcoming interpretation.

[Act Five] In the fifth act, the young King was told of all that had occurred between the Moor and his intended wife. First he made intercession for her with his father, pleading that she not be left in that condition. His

THE CHEMICAL WEDDING OF CHRISTIAN ROSENKREUZ

father agreed to it, and legates were made ready to comfort her in her sickness and imprisonment, yet also to reprimand her for her indiscretion. But she would not receive them, consenting instead to be the Moor's concubine; which also occurred, and the young King was informed of it.

[Fourth Interlude] Now came a chorus of fools, each of them carrying a piece out of which they rapidly assembled a great globe of the world, and immediately demolished it again. This was a fine entertaining fantasy.

[Sixth Act] In the sixth act, the young King decided to offer battle to the Moor, which took place, and the Moor was vanquished. Everyone thought that the young King was dead, too, but he recovered, freed his spouse, and prepared for his wedding, putting her under the guardianship of his steward and chaplain. The former greatly oppressed her until the tables were turned, and the padre became so bad and bold that he wanted all the power. When the young King was told of this, he instantly sent someone to break the padre's power, and to adorn the bride, in moderation, for the wedding.

[Fifth Interlude] After the act, a gigantic artificial elephant was brought out, which carried a great tower with musicians, to the delight of all.

[Act Seven] In the last act, the Bridegroom appeared with almost incredible pomp, so that I wondered how such things were possible. The Bride came toward him with great solemnity, and all the people cried out *"Vivat Sponsus: Vivat Sponsa"* [Long live the Bridegroom! Long live the Bride!] Thus, through the comedy, they were all congratulating our King and Queen in the most courtly manner. All of which, as I later learned, pleased them extraordinarily.

Finally they all circled round once in a procession, till at last everyone began to sing as follows:

I

This blessed time brings us such joy, with the King's wedding; therefore sing ye all and let it sound forth! Joy be his who bestows this on us.

II

The lovely Bride whom we have awaited so long will now be betrothed to him. We have won what we have striven for. Happy is he who looks to himself.

III

Now good parents are called for. She [the bride] has been long in tutelage. Increase honorably, that thousands may arise from your own blood.

After this they took their leave, and so the comedy, especially pleasing to the Royal Persons, came to a happy end. Evening had almost come, so everyone departed in the same order; but we were to follow the Royal Persons up the spiral stair to the chamber I have spoken of. Here the tables were richly set, and it was the first time that we had been invited to the royal table. The little altar was placed in the middle of the room, and the six royal insignia were laid upon it. The young King conducted himself very graciously toward us, but he could not have been entirely happy because, though he sometimes talked a little with us, he frequently sighed. Little Cupid only scoffed and played his tricks.

The old King and Queen were very serious, and only the wife of one of the old ones showed any levity; I did not know why. The first table was occupied by the Royal Persons, and we sat by ourselves at the second. At the third table were certain well-born maidens. All the other men and maidens had to wait. Everything was conducted with great state, but in such solemn stillness that I dare not say much about it. I must nonetheless mention that before the meal all the Royal Persons had put on shining snow-white clothing, and thus sat down at table. Above the table hung the same great golden crown, whose precious stones alone could well have sufficed to light the room. However, all the lights were kindled from the small taper on the altar: for what reason, I truly do not know. I certainly noticed that the young King several times sent food to the white snake on the altar, which also gave me something to think about. The chatter at this banquet was almost all young Cupid's, who could leave none of us alone, least of all myself, and was always coming up with some surprise. But there was no joy besides, and everything took place in silence. I could well imagine that some catastrophe was imminent. No music was to be heard; if any was asked a question, we replied in short, leaden words, and left it at that. In brief, everything had such a weird look about it that the sweat started to trickle down my body, and I think that the bravest man would have found his courage ebbing.

Now that this supper was almost at an end, the young King called for the book to be brought him from the altar, and opened it. Then he had an old man ask us once again whether we intended to stay by him for better or worse. We affirmed this, trembling, whereupon he asked us sorrowfully whether we would put our names to it. We had no choice but to consent, and so each had to stand up in turn and sign the book with his own hand. When this was done, the crystal fountain was brought forward, together with one very tiny glass, and all the Royal Persons drank from it, one after the other. Then it was handed to us, and so on to all the other people; and this was called the *Haustus Silentii* [Draught of Silence]. Hereupon all the Royal Persons gave us their hands, with the warning that if we did not henceforth stay by them, we would never see them again. At this our eyes truly ran over, but our President engaged herself solemnly on our behalf, which satisfied them.

Now a small bell was rung, at which the Royal Persons grew so pale that we almost despaired. Soon they were laying aside their white garments and dressing all in black; the whole hall was hung with black velvet, the floor covered with the same, and also the ceiling, this having

THE CHEMICAL WEDDING OF CHRISTIAN ROSENKREUZ

all been prepared beforehand. Next the tables were removed and everyone sat round on the bench, ourselves also putting on black garments. Our President, who had been out, returned, bringing with her six satin bandages with which she bound the eyes of the six Royal Persons. Now that they could see nothing more, the servants speedily brought six covered coffins in to the chamber and set them down, also placing a low black bench in the middle. Finally a tall man entered the room, black as coal, bearing in his hand a sharp ax.

First the old King was led to the bench, and his head was instantly struck off and wrapped in a black cloth. The blood, however, was caught in a great golden chalice and placed with him in the nearby coffin, which was covered and set aside. So it went with the others, till I thought it would be my turn next; but this did not occur, for as soon as the six Persons were beheaded, the black man began to leave. Another followed him, and just before the door he struck off the executioner's head, and brought it back together with the ax, both of which were laid in a small chest.

This seemed to me a very bloody wedding, but since I had no notion of what might happen next, I had to reserve judgment against the outcome. Our Virgin also told us to hold our peace, as some of us were getting faint-hearted and weeping. Then she said to us: "The life of these now rests in your hands; and if you follow me, you will see this death give life to many." With this she indicated that we should go to sleep, and give ourselves no further worry: they would surely receive their just reward. Thus she wished us all a good night, telling us that she herself must keep vigil with the corpses tonight. We consented, and each was led by his page to his own lodging. My page talked to me long and variously, which I remember well to this day, and again astonished me with his intelligence. When I finally realized that his intention was to lull me to sleep, I pretended to be sleeping soundly. But no sleep came to my eyes, and I could not forget the people who had been beheaded.

THE CHEMICAL WEDDING OF CHRISTIAN ROSENKREUZ

My lodging was situated facing the great lake, so that I could easily look out over it. The windows, too, were near the bed. At midnight, just as it had struck twelve, I suddenly noticed a great fire out on the lake. Frightened, I immediately opened the window to see what would transpire. Then I saw seven ships approaching from afar, all of them full of lights. Above each one floated a flame which moved hither and thither, sometimes sinking quite low, which I readily concluded must be the spirits of the beheaded. These ships gradually neared the shore, and each had but one man for crew. As soon as they came to land, I saw our Virgin going toward the ships with a torch, and after her the six covered coffins and the chest were each carried to a ship and stowed out of sight.

I woke my page, who thanked me much, since, having run about so much during the day, he would have slept right through this, though he knew all about it. As soon as the coffins were laid in the ships, all the lights were extinguished. The six flames traveled together over the lake, so that each ship had no more than a single warning light. There were also some hundreds of guards camped on the waterside, who dispatched our Virgin back into the castle, where she carefully bolted everything up again. From this I guessed that nothing further would happen tonight, but that I must await the coming day, and so we went to bed again. I was the only one of my companions whose room had faced the lake, and who had seen this. Now I was tired out, and fell asleep in the midst of my manifold speculations.

> [Note in Latin] *Here several lines are missing which cannot be filled out at will; hence the editor declines to replace them arbitrarily. What the missing passage had to say is obvious to him who can see.*

THE FIFTH DAY

The night was over, and the long awaited day had broken, when I hastily got out of bed, more out of curiosity to know what would happen than because I had slept enough. After I had dressed I descended the stairs as usual, but it was still too early; I found no one else in the hall, so I asked my page to take me around the castle a little, and show me something unusual. As always, he did this willingly, and led me without delay down some steps beneath the ground to a great iron door, on which the following words were affixed in great copper letters:

Hye lygt begraben Venus, dye schön Fraw, so manchen Hoen man umb glück, ehr, segen, und wolfart gebracht hatt.
[Here lies buried Venus, the fair woman who has undone many a great man in fortune, honor, blessing, and prosperity.]

I copied this and drew it on my writing tablet. After the door was opened, the page led me by the hand through a very dark passage until we came to a small door, which stood ajar. The page told me that it had first been opened yesterday when the coffins were taken out through it, and had not yet been locked. As we entered, I beheld the most precious thing ever created by Nature. This vault had no light but that of some enormous carbuncles; and it was, as I was informed, the King's Treasury. Of all the things I saw there, the most marvelous and extraordinary was a tomb that stood in the center, so rich that I wondered why it was not better guarded. The page answered that I should thank my planet, through whose influence I would now see some more things that no man had ever set eyes on, beside the King's household.

This tomb was triangular, having in the center a shiny copper vessel; the rest was of pure gold and precious stones. In the vessel stood an angel who held in his arms an unknown tree, from which fruits continually fell into the vessel. As soon as they dropped in, the fruits turned to liquid

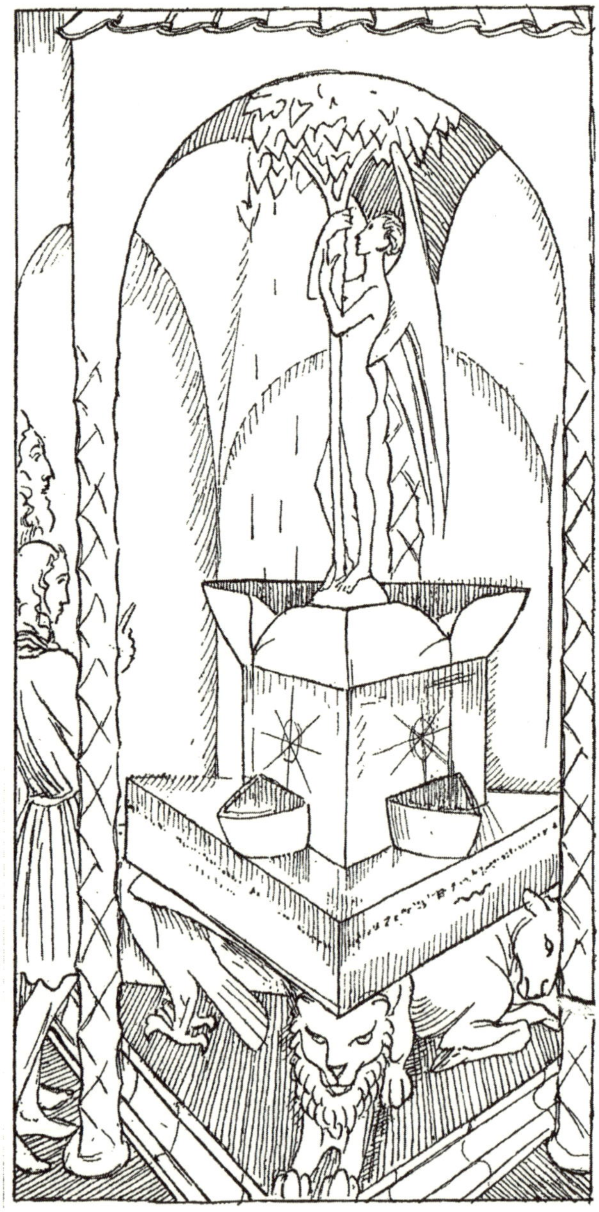

and flowed from there into three smaller golden vessels nearby. This little altar was supported by three beasts: Eagle, Ox, and Lion, all standing on a richly decorated base. I asked my page what this might mean: "Here lies buried Venus," he read, "the fair woman who has undone many a great man in fortune, honor, blessing, and prosperity." He then showed me a copper trapdoor in the floor; "Here," he said, "we could descend further if you would like to." "I am still following you," said I, and with that I went down the stairs. It was very dark, but the page quickly opened a little box in which was an ever-burning light; from this he lit one of the many torches that lay to hand. I was very scared, and asked him earnestly if he should be doing this. He answered me: "Since the Royal Persons are still asleep, I have nothing to fear."

Now I saw a rich bed, ready made, hung about with fine curtains of which he opened one. And there I beheld the Lady Venus quite naked (for he also lifted the covers), lying there in such magnificence and beauty that I was paralyzed. To this day I do not know whether it was a statue or a dead person lying there, for she was completely still, and I dared not touch her. Then she was covered up again and the curtain was drawn. I still had her in my mind's eye, until I noticed a tablet behind the bed on which was written:

Wan dye Frucht meynes baums wyrt vollends verscbmelzen, werde ych aufwachen und eyn muter seyn eynes konygs.
[When the fruit of my tree has completely melted, I shall awake and be the mother of a King.]

I asked my page about the inscription, but he laughed and promised that I would soon find out. Then he extinguished the torch and we climbed up again. Now that I could see all the little doors better, I found that at each corner a small pyrite taper was burning, which I had not noticed before, since the fire was so bright that it looked much more like a jewel than a

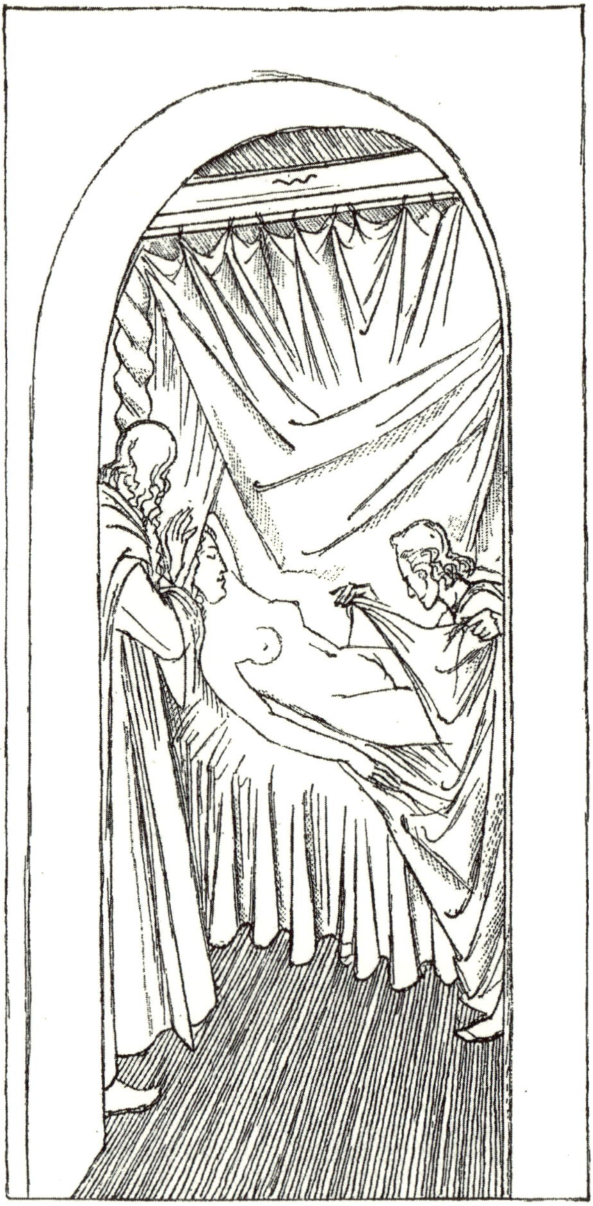

light. The tree must have been continually melting from their heat, yet it kept bringing forth more fruits. "Now," said the page, "learn what I have heard Atlas reveal to the King: when the tree has completely melted, the Lady Venus will wake up again and be the mother of a King."

As he was speaking, and perhaps was going to tell me more, little Cupid flew in. He was at first rather upset at our presence, but when he saw that we looked more dead than alive, he had to laugh. He asked me what spirit had led me here, to which I answered trembling that I had got lost in the castle, and somehow ended up here; that the page had been looking for me everywhere, and had finally found me; and that I hoped he would not hold it against me. "No, it's all right," said Cupid, "my nosy old father! But you could easily have played me a nasty trick if you'd noticed this door. I must take better care of it." And with this he put a strong padlock on the copper trapdoor through which we had climbed down.

I thanked God that he had not discovered us earlier, and my page was even gladder that I had thus helped him out. "I still can't let it go," said Cupid, "that you nearly stumbled across my dear mother." With that he held the point of his arrow in one of the tapers until it was warm, then pricked me on the hand. I thought little of it at the time, but was happy that we had succeeded in coming through without further danger.

Meanwhile my companions had also got out of bed and were in the hall. I joined them there, making as though I had just got up. After Cupid had carefully locked everything up, he also joined us and made me show him my hand. There was still a little drop of blood there, which much amused him, and he advised the others that they should look out for me: I would soon be growing old! We all wondered how Cupid could be so cheerful and give no thought to the tragic events of yesterday. But he showed no sign of sorrow.

In the meantime, our President had made herself ready for the journey. She entered all in black velvet, though still bearing her laurel branch, and all her maidens had laurel branches, too. Since everything was now ready, the Virgin told us first to take a drink, then to get ready for the procession without delay. We were not long about it, but followed her out of the hall into the courtyard. Here the six coffins were standing, and my companions had no other thought than that the six Royal Persons were lying within. I could see right through the trick, but still did not know what would be done with the others. By each coffin were eight masked men. As soon as the music began (and it was such grave and tragic music that I was awestruck), the men lifted up the coffins, and we followed after, as instructed, as far as the garden mentioned above.

A wooden building was erected in the middle, with a splendid crown around the roof, standing on seven columns. Inside were six open graves, with a stone by each, and in the center a tall, round, hollow stone. The coffins were laid in these graves, silently and with much ceremony, and the stones were slid over them and sealed fast. The little chest, however, was laid in the central one. My companions were deceived by this, for they quite thought that the corpses of the dead were inside. On top of all was a great banner with the Phoenix painted on it, perhaps the better to delude us. Here I had much to thank God for, because I had seen more than the rest.

After the burial was over, the Virgin mounted the central stone and made a short oration. She said that we should keep our promise, and, not grudging future pains, should help the Royal Persons thus entombed to come to life again. Therefore we were to rise up forthwith and go with her to Olympus Tower, to fetch from there the proper and indispensable medicines. We readily agreed, and followed her through another little door as far as the waterfront. There were the same seven ships, all empty, in which the maidens planted their laurel-branches, and after they had distributed us in the six ships, they sent us on our way in the name of God and watched us until we were out of sight. Then they went back into the castle with all the guards.

Each of our ships had a great banner and a special symbol. Five of them had the five *Corpora Regularia* [regular or Platonic solids], one apiece, while mine (in which the Virgin also sat) bore the sphere. We sailed in a special order, and each had only two crewsmen:

```
          a
       b  c  d
         e f
          g
```

In front went the little ship (a) in which I suspected the Moor lay, also containing twelve musicians who played very well; its symbol was a pyramid. Then came three abreast (b, c, d), in which we were, myself, in (c). In the middle went the two finest and stateliest ships (e, f); they had no one in them, but were trimmed with many laurel branches, and their banners were the sun and moon. Last (g) came a single ship in which were forty maidens.

After passing over the lake, we came through a narrow channel to the sea itself, where all the sirens, nymphs, and sea goddesses were awaiting us. A mermaid immediately came up to bring us their gift in honor of the wedding: it was a huge, precious, set pearl, round and lustrous, whose like has never been seen either in ours or in the New World. After the Virgin had graciously accepted it, the nymph asked her if we would anchor for a while and be an audience to their games; to which the Virgin also agreed. She had the two large ships heave to in the center, and the others make a pentagon around them:

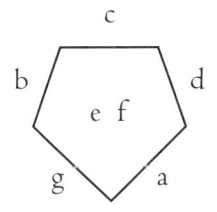

```
         c
      b     d
        e f
      g     a
```

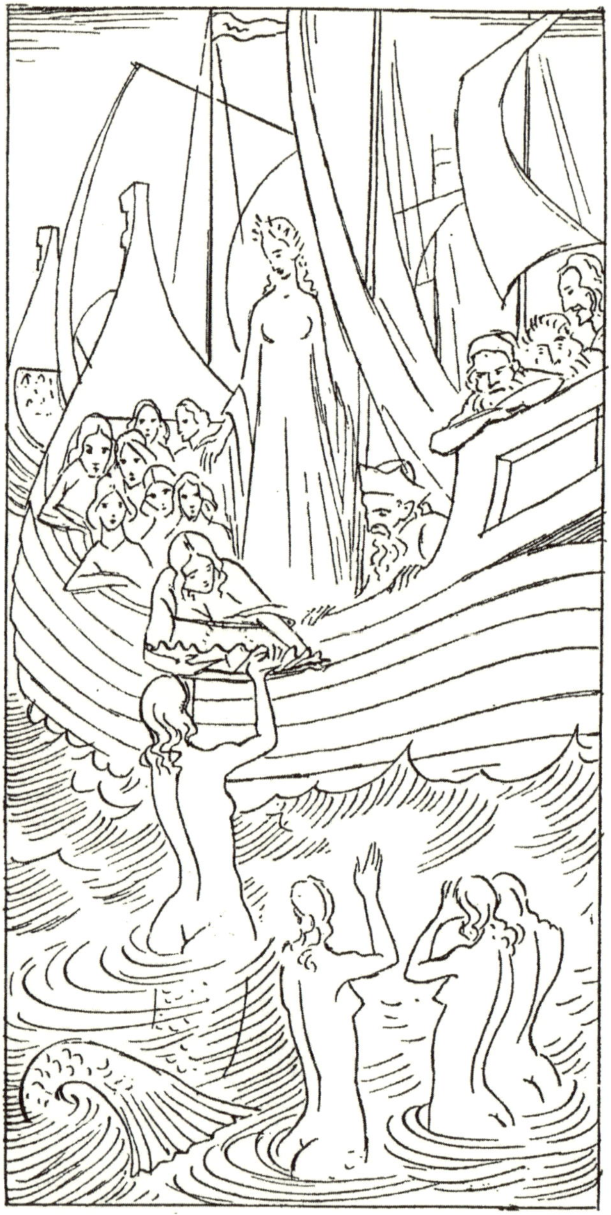

Then the nymphs swam round in a circle, singing with their lovely voices the following song:

I

On earth there's nothing better
Than fair and noble Love,
Through which we will turn godlike,
And none do other harm.
Therefore sing unto the King,
Make the whole sea to resound,
We ask you—answer us.

II

Who has brought us to life?
    'Tis Love.
Who has restored us grace?
    'Tis Love.
From whence have we our birth?
    From Love.
What could lead us astray?
    No Love.

III

Who has begotten us?
    'Twas Love.
Why did they give us suck?
    From Love.
What is our parents' due?
    Our Love.
Why are they patient so?
    From Love.

IV

What overcometh all?

    'Tis Love.

Can one find love as well?

    Through Love.

How can one do good work?

    In Love.

Who can unite the twain?

    'Tis Love.

V

So sing ye all,
Echoing loud,
In honor of Love,
Which will increase
Unto our lords the King and Queen;
Their bodies are here; their souls are gone.

VI

And while we live,
So God will grant
That as from us homage and love
Have sundered them with mighty power,
So may we too, through flame of love
With joy unite them once again.

VII

This sorrow, then,
To greatest joy,
Though many thousand generations come,
Shall be transformed for all eternity.

After they had finished this song with its beautiful words and melody, I no more wondered at Ulysses for having stopped his companions' ears, for I thought myself the most unhappy of men that nature had not made me an equally blissful creature. But the Virgin soon took her leave of them, and bade us sail away from there. Hence also the nymphs, after they had been presented with a long red ribbon in recompense, broke ranks and scattered in the sea.

At this time I became aware that Cupid was also beginning to work on me, which was really not to my credit; but since to tell of my deception would be of no use to the reader, I will let it go at that. It was the very head wound which I had received in my dream in the First Book. If any would be warned by me, let him not loiter around Venus's bed, for Cupid cannot abide that kind of thing.

After a few hours, when we had sailed a good way in friendly conversation, we espied Olympus Tower. Then the Virgin ordered some cannons to be fired as a sign of our arrival. Immediately we saw a great white flag run up, and a little golden boat coming toward us. When it arrived, there was an old gentleman, the Warder of the Tower, with some halberdiers dressed in white, by whom we were welcomed as friends and thus led to the Tower. This stood on a perfectly square island, surrounded by such a strong and thick rampart that I myself counted two hundred and sixty steps as we passed through it. Beyond the rampart was a fine meadow with some gardens, in which grew strange fruits unknown to me; then a wall around the Tower. The Tower itself was just as if seven round towers had been built together, but the central one was a little taller. They were all connected inside, and had seven stories.

As we came up to the gate of the Tower, they led us by the wall, a little off to the side. I could well see that it was so as to bring the coffins into the Tower without our knowledge, but the others knew nothing of this. As soon as it was done, they took us into the lowest part of the Tower. Although it was finely painted, we did not have much diversion

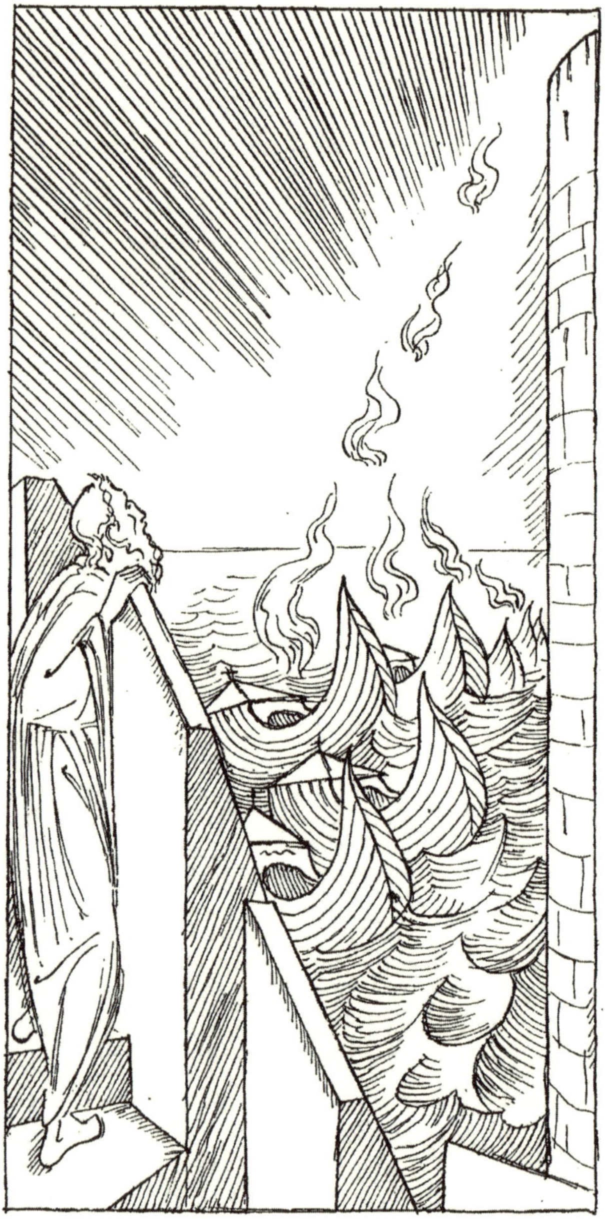

here, since this was nothing else than a laboratory. We had to grind and wash herbs, gemstones, and whatnot, extracting the sap and essence, then put it in little bottles and hand them over to be preserved. Our Virgin was so industrious and organizing, she knew how to keep each one fully employed. We had to drudge away on this island until we had done everything necessary for reviving the beheaded bodies. In the meantime (as I later learned), the three maidens were in the first room, and were diligently washing the corpses. Finally, as we were almost finished with these preparations, they gave us nothing but some broth and a sip of wine, from which I could see that we were not here for our amusement. Moreover, when we had finished our day's work, each one had only a quilt spread on the floor, and we had to make the best of it.

I was not much tempted to sleep, and so went out for a walk in the garden, coming eventually to the rampart. Since the skies were so clear, I could happily pass the time in contemplation of the stars. I accidentally came upon a great stone staircase, which led onto the rampart, and since the moon was shining very brightly, I was bold enough to go up and look a while over the sea, which was now utterly calm. Having such a good opportunity for astronomical observations, I discovered that on this very night there was a conjunction of planets such as would not be seen again for a long time.

After I had looked out to sea a good while, and it being around midnight, as soon as it had struck twelve I saw the seven flames coming from the distance over the sea until they reached the very top of the Tower. This somewhat frightened me, for as soon as the flames had come to land, the wind began to make the sea very rough. The moon was hidden by clouds, and my pleasure ended in such fear that I scarcely had time to find the staircase again and get back into the Tower. Whether the flames now stayed there, or whether they went away again, I cannot say, for I would never have dared venture out in such darkness. So I lay on my quilt and fell asleep all the sooner, since in our laboratory there was a fountain with a gentle murmuring sound. Thus the fifth day also ended with wonders.

THE SIXTH DAY

NEXT MORNING, after we had woken one another, we sat together a while to talk about what would come of all this. Some thought that they would all return to life together. Others, on the contrary, thought that the death of the old ones would afford the young ones not only life, but increase. Others again believed that they had not been killed, but that different people had been beheaded in their place. After we had discussed it together for some time, the old gentleman entered, greeted us, and looked around to see if all was ready and the procedures carried out sufficiently. Our conduct had been such that he could find no fault with our diligence, and so he collected all the glasses together and packed them in a case. Soon a few youths came in, bringing with them several ladders, ropes, and large wings which they laid down in front of us, and went out again. The old gentleman then began: "Dear sons, each must carry one of these three objects all day; but you are free either to choose one for yourselves, or to draw lots for them."

We said that we would like to choose. "No," replied the old gentleman, "it must be done by lot." Thereupon he made three tickets, on which he wrote respectively "Ladder," "Rope," and "Wings." These he placed in a hat, and each had to draw one, and that would be his. Those who got the ropes thought that they were best off, but I had a ladder, which annoyed me very much as it was twelve feet long and quite heavy. I had to carry it, whereas the others could wind their flexible ropes around themselves. For the third group, the old gentleman fixed on their wings as neatly as if they had grown there.

Now he turned off a tap, and the fountain stopped running; we then had to remove it from the middle of the room. After everything had been cleared away, he took the case with the glasses and left, locking the door fast after him, so that we could only think that we were imprisoned in this tower. But before a quarter of an hour had passed, a round hole was opened high up, and there we saw our Virgin, who called to us, wished us

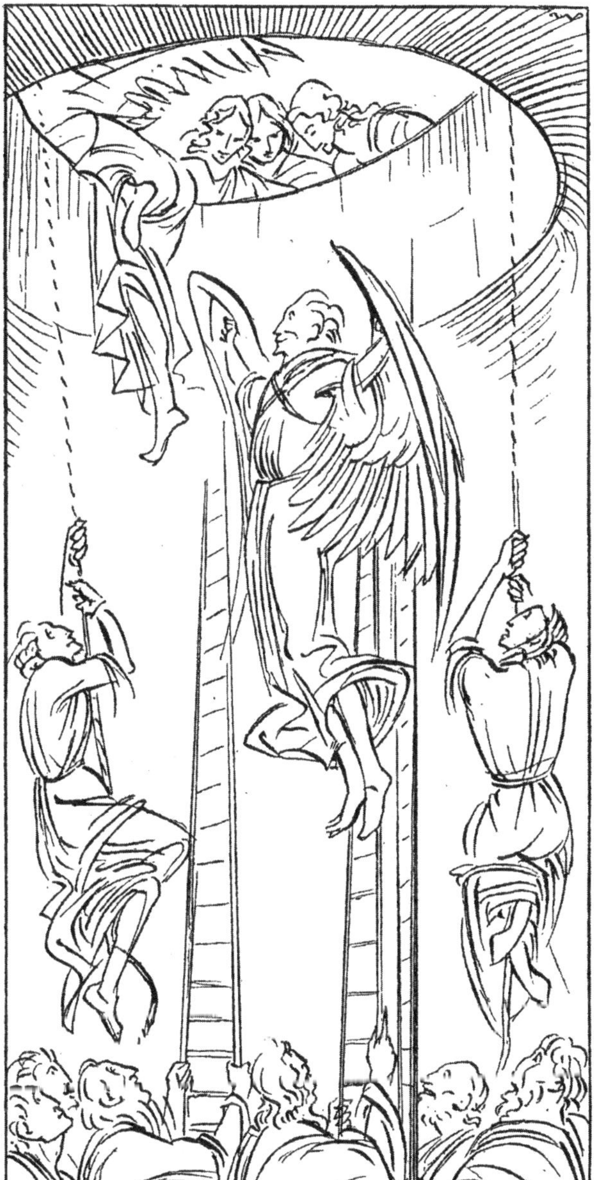

good day, and invited us to come up. The ones with wings were quickly through the opening, and we others soon saw what our ladders were for; only the ones with ropes were in trouble, for as soon as one of us arrived up there, he was told to draw his ladder up after him. At last each hung his rope on an iron hook, then had to climb up it, which was not to be done without blisters.

When we were all up, the opening was closed again and the Virgin gave us a kindly greeting. This room was as big as the tower and had six attractive chambers a little higher than the room, into which one had to climb by three steps. We were distributed in these chambers to pray for the lives of the King and Queen. Meanwhile the Virgin went in and out of the little door until we were ready.

As soon as we had finished our business, a peculiar, longish object was brought through the little door and placed in the middle by twelve persons (who had formerly been our musicians). My companions took it for a still, but I could well see that the corpses lay inside it, for the chest beneath it was rectangular, and easily big enough for six persons to lie inside. Then they went out again, fetched their instruments, and accompanied our Virgin and her maidservants with beautiful music.

The Virgin carried a little chest, the rest only branches and small lamps, and some of them lighted torches. Then we were also given torches to hold, and were made to stand around the fountain.

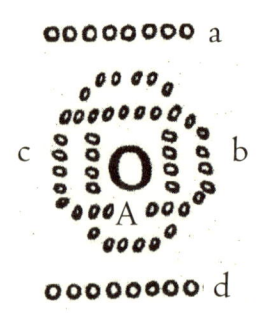

oooooooo a

c ⭕ b
A

oooooooo d

First stood the Virgin (A) with her maids around her in a circle, with their lamps and branches (c); then we stood with the torches (b); next the musicians were in a row (a), and the other maidens also in a row (d). I did not know where these maidens had come from: whether they lived in the Tower, or whether they had been brought there in the night, for all their faces were hidden with fine white veils, so that I could not recognize any of them.

Now the Virgin opened the little chest, in which was a round object wrapped in thick green satin. She laid this in the upper vessel, and covered it with a lid that was full of holes, and had a rim on which she poured some of the fluids that we had prepared yesterday. The still immediately began to flow, the liquid running back into the little vessel through four tubes. Under the lower vessel were many spikes on which the maidens hung their lamps, so that the heat came into the vessel and made the water simmer. When the water boiled, there were many small holes through which it could fall in on the corpses, and it was so hot that it dissolved all the bodies and turned them to liquid. My companions did not yet know what the round, wrapped-up thing above was, but I understood that it was the Moor's head, from which the water took on such extreme heat. Around the large vessel there were many holes in which the branches were stuck, though I did not know whether this was necessary, or just a ritual. However, these branches were continually sprinkled by the still, and the drips that returned from them into the vessel were somewhat more yellow.

The still had been running of its own accord for nearly two hours, but more feebly the longer it went. In the meantime the musicians broke ranks, and we walked about in the room, which was so set up that we had ample means of passing the time. Nothing had been omitted in the way of images, paintings, clocks, organs, running fountains, and the like. At last it came to the point at which the still would run no longer, whereupon the Virgin had a round golden sphere brought in. At the bottom of the still was a tap, through which she let all the matter that had been dissolved by those hot drops run into the sphere, a portion of which was very red. The other water remained above in the vessel, and was poured out. Then this still, which had now become much lighter, was taken out again. I myself cannot say whether it was opened outside, or whether anything further of value remained of the corpses; but I do know that the water that was collected in the sphere was much heavier, for it took six or more of us to carry it, though by its size it should not have been too heavy for one.

After this sphere had with difficulty been taken out through the door, we were left sitting alone again, but when I heard a coming and going above us, I had an eye to my ladder. One would have heard my companions give strange opinions about this still, for since they could not imagine the corpses to be anywhere but in the castle garden, they could not evaluate this process. But I thanked God that I had woken at such an opportune time, and seen that which helped me better in everything the Virgin did.

After a quarter of an hour the cover above us was opened, and we were commanded to come up, which we did as before with wings, ladders, and ropes. It annoyed me somewhat that the maidens must have gone up by another way, while we had to work so hard; but I realized that there was something special about it, and also that we had to leave the old gentleman something to do. Even those with wings had no advantage, except when they came to pass through the opening. When we had got up there, and the aperture had been closed, I saw the sphere in the middle of the room, hanging by a strong chain.

There was nothing in this room but plain windows, and between each pair of them a door, which concealed nothing but a great polished mirror. These windows and mirrors were placed opposite each other for optical effect, such that when the sun (now shining more brightly than usual) met just one of the doors, nothing but sun was visible throughout the whole room, so long as the window facing the sun was open, and the doors in front of the mirrors likewise. Through artificial reflection they all shone onto the golden sphere which hung in the center, and since this too was highly polished, it gave off such a blaze that none of us could keep his eyes open. We had to look out of the windows until the sphere was well heated and the desired effect achieved. Here I must say that in this mirroring I beheld the most wonderful thing that Nature ever brought to light: for everywhere there were suns, but the sphere in the center shone even brighter, so that like the sun we could not bear to look at it for a moment.

At last the Virgin commanded the mirrors to be closed again and the windows shut, so that the sphere could cool off a little; and this occurred toward seven o'clock. We thought this was good, since we could now have a vacation and refresh ourselves a little with breakfast. But this collation was extremely philosophical, and we had no need to worry about intemperance—yet we were not starved. The hope of coming joy, with which the Virgin continually reassured us, made us so happy that we gave no heed to labor or inconvenience. I can also say this truly of my illustrious companions: that they never thought of kitchen or table, but their pleasure was only in the pursuit of such adventurous physics, and in the contemplation therein of the Creator's wisdom and omnipotence.

After we had taken our meal, we settled down to work again, for the sphere had sufficiently cooled. With great trouble and difficulty we had to lift it off the chain and onto the floor. Now came the debate over how we were to divide it, because our instructions were to cut it apart in the middle. In the end, a sharp diamond turned out to be best. When we opened the sphere, there was nothing red inside it, but a beautiful, large, snow-white egg. It pleased us immensely that it had turned out so well, for the Virgin was always worrying that the shell might still be too fragile. We stood around this egg with as much joy as if we had laid it ourselves! But the Virgin soon had it removed, disappeared herself, and as always locked the door. I do not know whether she did something out there with the egg, or whether something clandestine was done to it, but I do not believe so. We, however, had to wait by ourselves for a quarter of an hour until the third hole was opened, and we came by means of our apparatus to the fourth story or floor.

In this chamber we found a great copper vessel filled with yellow sand, warmed by a gentle fire, in which the egg was buried so as to come to full maturity. This vessel was square, and on one side these two verses were written in large letters:

O.BLI.TO.BIT.MI.LI.
KANT.I.VOLT.BIT.TO.GOLT.

On the other side were these three words:

SANITAS. NIX.HASTA.
[Health; Snow; Lance]

The third had nothing but the single word:

F.I.A.T.
[So be it]

But on the back was a whole inscription, reading as follows:

QUOD.
Ignis: Aer: Aqua: Terra:
SANCTIS REGUM ET REGINARUM NOSTR:
Cineribus
Eripere non potuerunt .
Fidelis Chymicorum Turba.
IN HANC URNAM
Contulit.
Ad .

[What Fire, Air, Water, Earth, could not rob from the holy ashes of our Kings and Queens, the faithful flock of alchemists has gathered in this urn. AD 1459.]

I leave it for the learned to argue about whether the sand or the egg was meant by this. I will do my part and leave nothing unsaid. Now our egg was ready, and was taken out. It needed no cracking, for the bird inside soon extracted itself, and appeared quite happy although it looked very bloody and unformed. We placed it first on the warm sand, and the Virgin said that before anything was given it to eat, we should tie it up, otherwise it would give us all trouble aplenty. This was done, and then food was brought to it, which was surely none other than the blood of the beheaded people, diluted again with prepared water.

The bird grew so fast beneath our very eyes that we could understand why the Virgin had warned us about it: it bit and scratched about itself so fiercely that if anyone had fallen into its clutches it would soon have done away with him. Now it was quite black and wild, and so another food was brought for it—perhaps the blood of another Royal Person— whereupon all the black feathers fell out again, and in their place there grew snow-white plumage. Then it became somewhat tamer and easier to deal with, though we still did not trust it. With the third meal, its feathers began to become colored, and so beautiful that in all my life I have never seen colors to compare. By now the bird was extremely docile and so friendly toward us that with the Virgin's consent we let it out of captivity.

"Now," she began, "since through your hard work and our old gentleman's permission the bird has been endowed with life and great perfection, it is proper for us to give it a joyful consecration." Thereupon she ordered lunch to be brought in, and us to relax, since now the most demanding work was over and it was fitting for us to enjoy our past labors. We began to be merry together, though we still had on our mourning

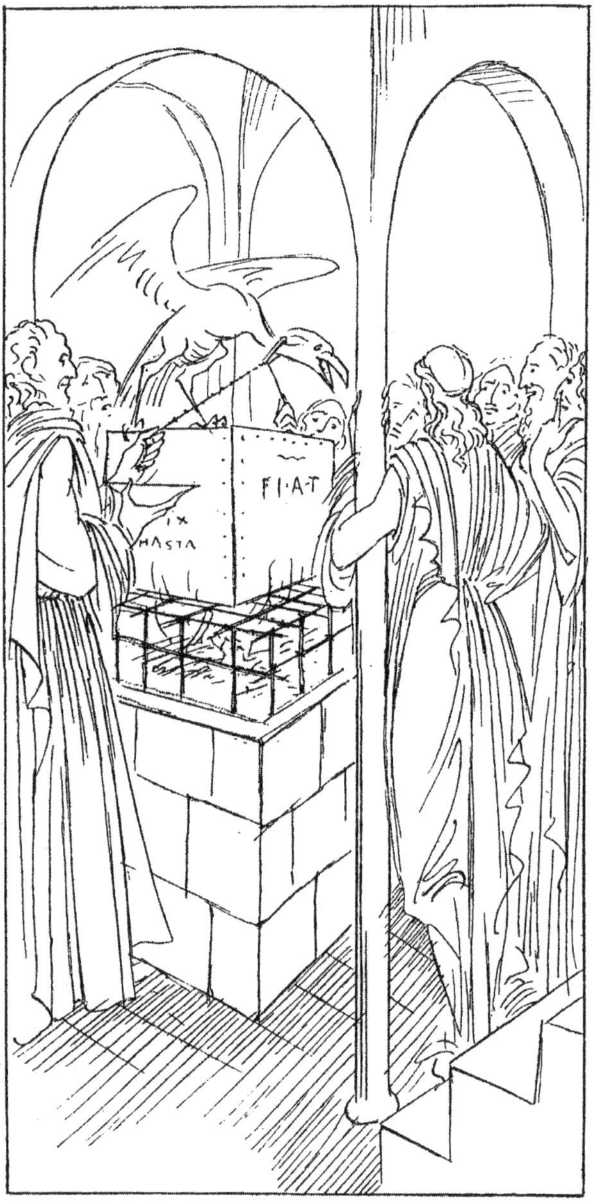
FI·A·T
IX
HASTA

clothes, which seemed to make rather a mockery of our joy. The Virgin kept asking questions, perhaps to find out which of us would be best served by her forthcoming scheme. She was mostly concerned with smelting, and was very pleased when she found someone adept at the fine manipulations which distinguish an artist. This luncheon lasted no longer than three-quarters of an hour, most of which we spent with our bird, which we constantly had to feed with its food; but now it stayed the same size.

We were not left very long to digest our meal, but after the Virgin had gone away, together with the bird, the fifth chamber was opened to us, where we offered our services after getting there in the accustomed way. In this room, a bath was prepared for our bird, colored with a fine white powder so as to look like pure milk. It was cool at first, and when the bird was put in it enjoyed it, drinking out of it and playing around. But then it began to be heated by the lamps placed underneath, and we had trouble keeping the bird in the bath. So we clapped a lid on the vessel, but let it stick its head out through a hole. In this bath it shed all its feathers and became as smooth as a human being; also the heat no longer hurt it. This amazed me, since all its feathers were consumed in this bath, coloring the water blue.

At length we gave the bird air, and it sprang out of the vessel by itself, so shining smooth that it was a delight to see. But since it was still somewhat wild, we had to put a collar with a chain round its neck, and thus led it up and down the room. Meanwhile, a strong fire was lit under the vessel, and the bath was boiled away until it turned all to a blue stone, which we took out and crushed; then we had to grind it on a stone, and finally paint the bird's skin all over with the resulting color. Now it looked stranger still, for it was blue all over except for its head, which stayed white.

Now all our work on this floor was completed, so after the Virgin had left with our blue bird, we were summoned through the opening to the sixth floor, whither we went. Here we were much troubled, for in the middle there stood an altar, exactly as described above in the King's hall; on it stood the six objects I have mentioned, and the bird itself made a seventh. First the little fountain was set before it, from which it drank a good draught. Then it pecked the white snake until it was badly bleeding. We had to collect this blood in a golden beaker, and pour it down the throat of the bird, who resisted violently. Next we dipped the snake's head into the fountain, so that it came back to life and crept into its skull, after which I saw nothing of it for a long time.

Meanwhile, the sphere was moving ever forward until it made the desired conjunction, and the little clock immediately struck one. Thereupon followed another conjunction, and the clock struck two. Finally, as we observed the third conjunction and it was signaled by the clock, the poor bird submissively laid its neck on the book, and willingly allowed its head to be struck off by one of us, chosen for this by lot. It gave forth not a drop of blood until its breast was opened, when the blood spurted out as fresh and clear as if it had been a fountain of rubies.

Its death touched us to the heart, yet we could not imagine that a mere bird would help us much, so we let it be. We cleared it off the altar and helped the Virgin burn it to ashes, together with the small tablet hanging nearby, with fire lit from the taper. The ashes were purified several times and carefully preserved in a box of cypress wood.

Here I cannot conceal what a trick was played on me and three others. After we had carefully put away the ashes, the Virgin began thus:

"Dear sirs, we are now in the sixth chamber, and have only one more before us, in which our labors will be at an end; we will travel back to our castle, to awaken our most gracious Lords and Ladies. I would have wished that all of you, gathered together here, had conducted yourselves in such a way that I could have commended you to our most worthy King and Queen, and that you might have received a fitting reward. But these four (here she pointed to me and three others) have proved, against my wishes, to be lazy and indolent workers.

"However, because of my charity toward one and all, I do not want to deliver them to their well-deserved punishment; yet so that such idleness shall not remain wholly unpunished, I propose this for them: they alone shall be excluded from the forthcoming seventh operation, the most wondrous of all; but they will not need to make further atonement afterward, before Their Majesties."

I leave others to imagine how I felt after this speech, for the Virgin was able to look so serious that the floods overflowed and we thought ourselves the most miserable of all men. Then the Virgin had the musicians called by one of the maidservants (of whom there were always many at hand), and they with their cornetts had to play us out of the door, with such mockery and derision that they could scarcely blow for laughing. What hurt us especially was that the Virgin herself found our tears, anger, and anxiety so amusing, and that among our companions there may have been some who enjoyed our discomfiture.

But it turned out quite differently. For as soon as we were out of the door, the musicians told us to cheer up and follow them up the spiral stair that led past the seventh story to beneath the roof. There we found the old gentleman, whom we had not seen hitherto, standing by a little round furnace. He received us kindly and congratulated us heartily on being thus chosen by the Virgin. But when he understood the fright we had received, he almost burst himself laughing at us for having taken our good fortune so ill. "So, dear sons, learn from this," he said, "that man never knows what good things God intends for him."

As he was speaking, the Virgin came calmly in with her box, and after she was done laughing at us, she emptied the ashes into another container, and filled hers up again with a different substance, explaining that she must now throw some sand in the other artists' eyes; but that we should do as the old gentleman told us, and especially not let our efforts flag. Thereupon she left us for the seventh room, into which she summoned our companions. What she first did with them there, I cannot tell, for not only were they strictly forbidden to say, but because of our duties we did not dare to spy on them through the ceiling. Our work was as follows: we had to saturate the ashes with our previously prepared water until they became a thin paste. Then we set the material on the fire until it was well heated. While it was hot, we poured it out into two little forms or molds, and let it cool slightly.

Now we had a moment to spy on our companions through some cracks. They were busy with an oven, each one having to blow the fire himself with a pipe. Around they stood, blowing fit to burst, but still thinking it wonderful how much better off they were than us. This blowing went on so long that our old gentleman called us back to work, so I do not know what happened afterward.

We opened up the molds, and there were two beautiful, bright, and almost transparent images such as human eyes have never seen, of a little boy and girl, each only four inches long. What amazed me the most was that they were not hard, but as soft and flesh-like as any human being; but they had no life. I am quite certain that the Lady Venus's image was made in some such way. These babies, lovely as angels, we laid first on two satin cushions, and gazed at them for a long time, reduced to idiocy by such an enchanting spectacle. But the old gentleman roused us and told us continually to let one drop after another of the bird's blood, which had been caught in the golden beaker, fall into the images' mouths. This apparently made them grow, and whereas they had started out tiny, now they grew more beautiful in proportion to their size. Would that all painters could have been here, to be ashamed of their art in the face of these creations of Nature!

Now they were getting so big that we lifted them off the cushions and had to lay them on a long table covered with white velvet, as the old gentleman directed us, and covered them as far as the chest with a soft white satin sheet. They were so inexpressibly beautiful that we did this almost reluctantly. In short, before we had used up all the blood, they

THE CHEMICAL WEDDING OF CHRISTIAN ROSENKREUZ

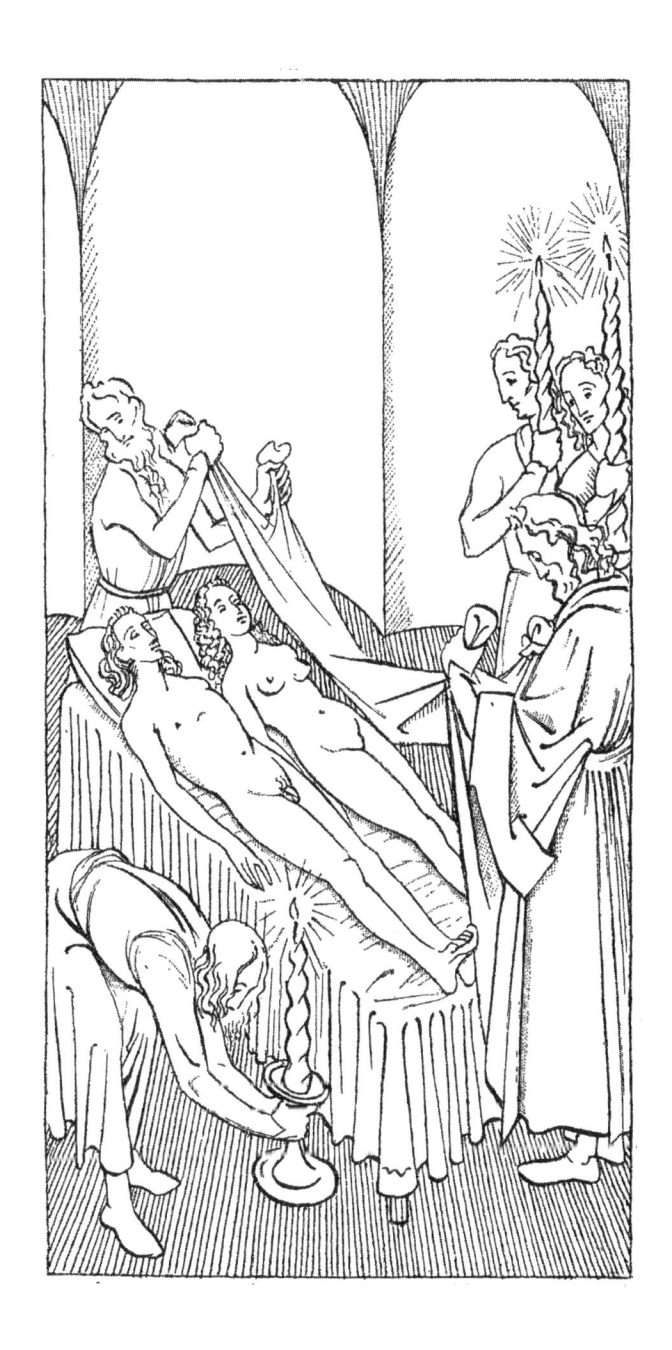

were already fully grown, and both had curly golden-yellow hair. The image of Venus was nothing to them. But there was no natural warmth there, no feeling; they were dead images, yet lively and natural in color. For fear that they might grow too big, the old gentleman had them fed no more, but pulled the sheet up over their faces and had the table stuck around with torches.

Here I must warn the reader not to think of these lights as necessary, for the old gentleman's intention was merely that we should not see when the souls went into them. We would not have noticed it, if I had not twice before seen the flames; but I let the other three rest in their belief, nor did the old gentleman know that I had seen anything more.

Hereupon he asked us to sit down on a bench opposite the table, and presently the Virgin came in with the musicians and all the apparatus. She carried two beautiful white garments of a sort I had never seen in the castle, nor can I describe them, for I could only think that they were of pure crystal, only soft and opaque. That is all I can say about them. She laid them down on a table, and after setting her maidens around on the bench, she and the old gentleman began to do a lot of conjuring round the table, which was only to confuse us. This happened, as I have said, under the roof, which was made in a remarkable way: inside there were seven concave hemispheres; the middle one was somewhat higher and had at the top a small round hole which was closed, and which none of the others had observed.

After much ceremony six maidens came in, each carrying a large trumpet that was wound round with a green, fiery, luminous material, like a wreath. The old gentleman took one of them, and after removing some of the lights at the head of the table and uncovering the faces, he set a trumpet in one of the mouths so that the upper and wider part came exactly to the roof-vent. My companions were staring only at the bodies, but I had other thoughts, for as soon as the foliage or wreath around the tube was kindled, I saw the hole above open and a bright stream of fire shoot through the tube and pass into the body. Then the hole was shut again and the trumpet removed, through which trick my companions were deceived into thinking that life had entered the image through the fire of the foliage. As soon as the soul was received, the body opened and closed its eyes, but scarcely moved. Again he placed another tube on its mouth, lit it, and the soul was let down through the tube; and this happened three times to each. Then all the lights were extinguished and removed, the velvet tablecloth folded over the bodies, and a folding bed set up and prepared, on which the wrapped bodies were placed. They were taken out of the coverings, laid neatly side by side, and left to sleep a good while with the curtains drawn.

Now it was time for the Virgin to see how our other artists were faring. They were quite happy, for, as the Virgin later told me, they were having to work in gold (which is also a part of this art, though not the noblest, the most necessary, or the best). They also had a portion of these ashes, and were firmly convinced that the whole bird was provided for the sake of gold, and that thus the dead bodies would be brought back to life. Meanwhile we sat silently waiting for our couple to awaken, which took place after about half an hour. Now cheeky Cupid came in again and, after greeting each of us, flew in under the bed-curtain and pestered them until they awoke. This caused them great astonishment, for they thought that they had simply slept from the moment they were beheaded until now. Cupid, after he had woken them and introduced them to one another again, stepped aside a little and let the two of them recover somewhat. Then he aimed his tricks at us, and in the end we were obliged to fetch the musicians for him and to be more cheerful. Not long afterward the Virgin herself entered, and after she had humbly greeted the young King and Queen (who still felt rather weak), and kissed their hands, she brought them the two beautiful garments I mentioned, which they put on and thus stepped forward. Now two fine seats had been made ready, and there they sat, to be greeted by us with the deepest submission. The King, in his own person, most graciously thanked us and again assured us of his favor.

It was already about five o'clock, and they could not stay longer, but as soon as the most important things could be loaded, we led the young Royal Persons down the spiral staircase, through all the doors and guards, to the ship. There they embarked together with some of the maidens and Cupid, and sailed away so swiftly that we soon lost sight of them. But I was told that they were met by many stately ships, and that in four hours they had traversed many miles of sea.

After five o'clock, the musicians were told to take everything back onto the ships, and to prepare for departure. But since it was going rather slowly, the old gentleman for the first time brought out some of his secret soldiers, who up to now had been hidden in the ramparts so that we had seen none of them. From this I could tell that the Tower was well provided against opposition. These soldiers made short work of our stuff, so there was soon no more to be done than to eat supper.

The table was already set, as the Virgin brought us back to our companions. We had to look downcast and keep from laughing, but they smiled at one another, though a few of them were sorry for us. The old gentleman was also with us at supper, and a keen inspector he was; none could say anything so clever that he would not either turn it around, or cap it, or at least give some good information about it. I learnt a great deal from this gentleman, and it would be excellent if everyone were to go to him and learn his business, then things would often not turn out so badly.

After we had eaten supper, the old gentleman led us first into his cabinets of curiosities here and there in the bastions. There we saw such marvels of Nature, and other things imitated from Nature by the human mind, that even a year would not have sufficed us. We examined them by lamplight far into the night. At last, when we desired sleep more than seeing any further strange thing, we were led to our quarters and there, in the rampart, had not only fine, comfortable beds but unusually elegant rooms. This made us wonder all the more why we had been made to suffer so yesterday. I slept well in my bedroom, and since I was largely unworried, and weary from constant working, the soft rushing of the sea helped me to a sound and gentle sleep, and I continued in a dream from eleven o'clock at night until eight in the morning.

THE SEVENTH DAY

I WOKE AFTER eight o'clock and quickly got myself ready, intending to go back to the Tower. But the dark passages in the rampart were so many and various that I wandered a good while before finding an exit. This happened to others, too, until at last we met in the lowest vault and were given clothes all of yellow, as well as our Golden Fleeces. At this time the Virgin told us that we were Knights of the Golden Stone, which we had not known beforehand. When we were all ready and breakfasted, the old gentleman presented each one with a golden medal, on one side of which were these words:

AR.NAT.MI.
[*Ars naturae ministra:* Art is the minister of Nature]

On the other side were these:

TEM.NA.F.
[*Temporis natura filia:* Nature is the daughter of Time]

He exhorted us to take nothing over and beyond these mementos. Then we went out to the sea again, where our ships lay, so splendidly appointed that it was scarcely possible; such beautiful things must have been brought there beforehand. There were twelve ships: six of ours and six of the old gentleman's, the latter all manned with smartly turned-out soldiers. He himself came on our ship, where we were all together. In the first sat the musicians, of which the old gentleman had a great number,

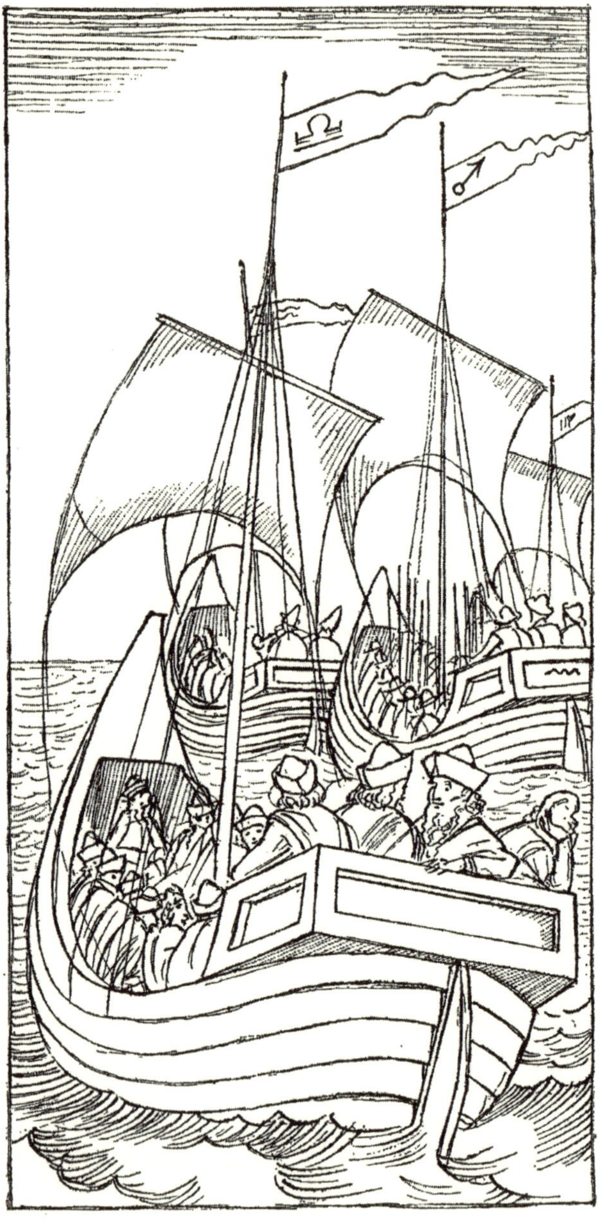

sailing in front of us to make the time pass more pleasantly. Our flags were the twelve signs of the zodiac, and we were in Libra. Among other things, our ship had a very lovely clock, which showed all the minutes; and the sea was so calm that it was a great pleasure to sail on it. Best of all was the old gentleman's discourse. He told us wonderful stories to pass the time, so that I could happily have traveled with him my life long. Meanwhile the ships went quite speedily, and before two hours had passed, the sailor told us that he could already see almost the whole lake covered with ships, from which we guessed that they were expecting us. As soon as we left the sea and came through the channel into the lake, there were about five hundred vessels, among them one sparkling with pure gold and gemstones in which sat the King and Queen with many noble lords, ladies, and maidens.

As soon as they saw us, all the cannons on both sides were fired, and there was such a din of trombones, trumpets, and kettledrums that all the ships on the lake shuddered. Finally, as we arrived they surrounded our ships and we hove to. Straightway, old Atlas came aboard on the King's behalf, made a short but eloquent speech in which he bade us welcome, and asked whether the royal gift was ready. My other companions wondered greatly how this King had resurrected, for they thought that they would have to reawaken him. But we left them in their confusion and made as if we did not understand, either. After Atlas' speech, our old gentleman came forward and responded with a somewhat longer oration, in which he wished the King and Queen all joy and increase, then handed over a small decorated casket. But what was in it, I did not know. Cupid alone was entrusted with it, as he flitted around between the two of them. When the speech was over, a salvo was fired, and we sailed together for a while until at last we came to another waterfront.

This was near the first gate, by which I had originally entered. On the square a great crowd of the royal household was waiting, together with several hundred horse. As soon as we docked and landed, the King and Queen offered each of us their hand with especial courtesy, and we were

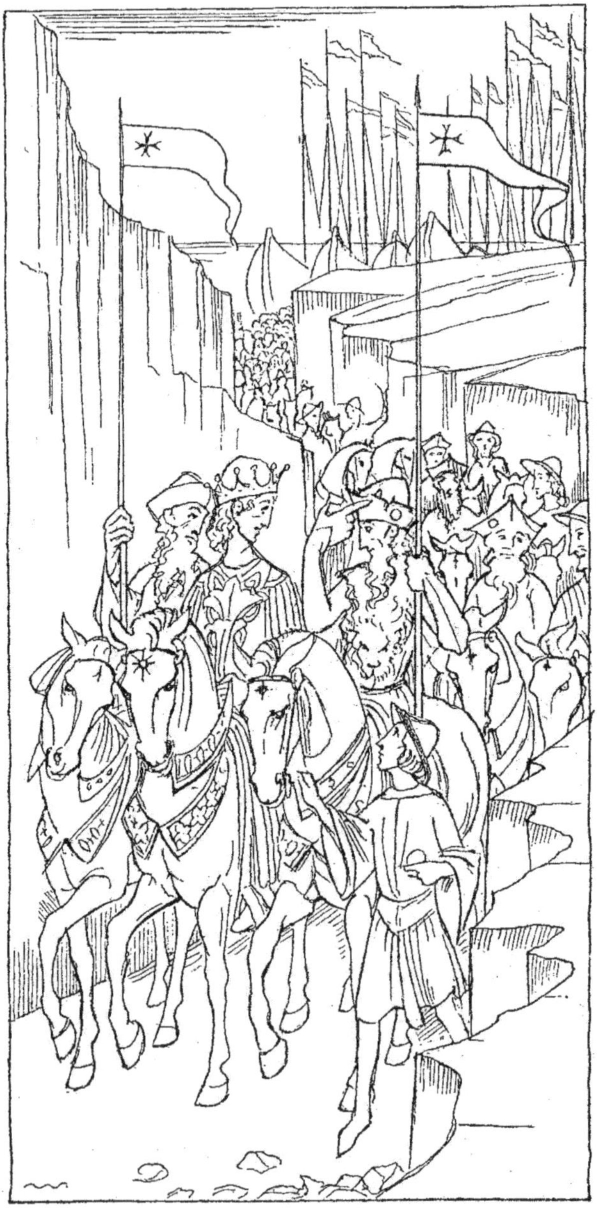

all mounted on horseback. Here I would ask my friendly reader not to take this narrative as pride or self-glorification, but to believe that if it were not strictly necessary, I would much prefer to have kept silent about the honor shown to me. We were all distributed among the Lords, but our old gentleman and my unworthy self had to ride beside the King, each of us carrying a snow-white standard with a red cross. My treatment was surely due to my age, for both of us had long gray beards and hair. I had fastened my tokens around my hat, which the young King soon noticed, asking whether I was the one who was able to redeem the tokens beneath the portal. I answered humbly "Yes"; but he laughed at me, and told me I should need no decoration from now on: I was his father! Then he asked me what I had redeemed them with. I answered "with water and salt," whereupon he asked who had made me so wise. Then I grew bolder and told him what had happened with my bread, the dove, and the raven. He was pleased, but said expressly that God must have given me extraordinarily good fortune in this.

Now we came to the first portal, where the blue-clad porter stood holding a petition in his hand. As soon as he saw me beside the King he handed me the petition, humbly entreating that I would remind the King of the porter's kindness to me. First I asked the King how it stood with this porter. He answered me in a friendly way that he used to be a famous and skilled astrologer, held in great honor by the King's father, but that he had once offended the Lady Venus, and seen her in her bed. As punishment for this he was made to guard the first portal until someone should release him from it. I asked whether he could now be released. The King said: "Yes, if someone can be found who has committed as great a sin as he; they can take his place, and he will be free."

These words cut me to the quick, for my conscience convinced me that I was the offender. But I kept silent and handed over the petition. As soon as the King had read it, he was so alarmed that the Queen, who was riding behind us with her maidens and another Queen (whom I remembered from the hanging of the weights), noticed it and asked him what this letter meant. But he had not wanted anything to be noticed, and, putting away the letter, began to talk of other things until we came to the castle at about three o'clock.

When we had dismounted and accompanied the King into his hall, he called old Atlas to join him in a small closet and showed him the letter. Atlas lost no time in riding back to the porter, to find out more about this matter. The young King sat down with his wife and other lords, ladies, and maidens. Then our Virgin began to praise loudly our diligence, trouble, and labors, with the request that we be royally rewarded, and that she might enjoy the benefit of her commission from then on. The old gentleman also stood up and, confirming all that the Virgin had spoken, said that it would be only just for us all to receive satisfaction. Now we were told to step out for a while, and each to make a feasible wish, which would be granted; for there was no doubt that the wisest would make the best wish. We were to think about it until after dinner.

Now the King and Queen began to play a game with each other, to pass the time. It resembled chess, but had different rules: it was between the Virtues and the Vices, and it was pretty to see what traps the Vices set for the Virtues, and how they could be countered. The game was so clever and ingenious that I wished we had it, too. During the game, Atlas returned and delivered his message secretly. I went red from head to foot, for my conscience left me no peace. The King told me to read the petition for myself, whose contents were roughly as follows: first, the porter wished the King prosperity and increase, that his seed should be spread far and wide. Then he indicated that the day had now come when, according to the royal promise, he should be relieved. If his observations did not deceive him, Venus had already been discovered by one of his guests. If His Majesty would make keen and diligent inquiry, he would find that his discovery was true; and if none such were to be found, he would remain by the gate for the rest of his life. He then requested most humbly that if, in peril of his life and limb, he were permitted to attend dinner tonight, he would hope to identify the miscreant himself and thus earn the freedom he desired. All this was explicitly and eloquently put, so that I could well appreciate the porter's ingenuity; but it was too painful for me, and I would prefer never to have set eyes on it. I wondered whether I could help myself out of it through my wish, so I asked the King whether the porter could be released in any other way. "No," answered the King, "for there is a special consideration in this matter; but we may well concede his request for this evening. Send someone out to fetch him here." Meanwhile, tables were being set in a room where we had never been before: it was so perfect and well furnished that I cannot begin to describe it. We were conducted in with particular pomp and ceremony. Cupid was not here this time, for, as I learned, he was rather angry at the affront his mother had received. In short, my action and the porter's petition were a matter for great sorrow. The King hesitated to institute an enquiry among all his guests, for then those who knew nothing of the matter would find out about it. So as soon as the porter arrived, he let the man himself look sharply around him, while the King behaved as cheerfully as he could.

At last people began to be merrier, and to make all kinds of interesting and diverting conversation. There is no need to tell the reader all about the feast and other ceremonies, for that is not what I intend; but everything was beyond measure, thanks more to art and human skill than to the fact that we had drunk heavily. This was the last and most splendid meal we had attended. After the banquet, the tables were quickly cleared and some elegant chairs put round in a circle in which we were to sit, together with the King and Queen, the two old men, the ladies and maidens. A handsome page now opened the wonderful little book mentioned earlier. Atlas placed himself in the midst and began to read from it to us, to the effect that His Majesty had not forgotten what we had done for him, and how diligently we had discharged our duties; therefore, as a reward, he appointed each and every one of us a Knight of the Golden Stone. We were to note that henceforth we must not only submit to His Majesty, but hold to the following articles; thus His Majesty would also know how to behave toward his liegemen. Then Atlas had the page read the articles, which were these:

1. You Lord Knights shall swear to ascribe your Order not to any devil or spirit, but only to God your Creator, and to Nature, his handmaiden.

2. You shall abominate all whoredom, incontinence, and uncleanness, and not defile your Order with such vices.

3. Through your gifts you shall willingly come to the aid of all who are deserving and in need.

4. You shall not desire this honor to use it for worldy show or high esteem.

5. You shall not wish to live longer than God wills.

We had to laugh at this last article, which was perhaps put in only as a joke. We now had to swear to them all on the King's scepter, then we were installed as Knights with the customary rites, and among other privileges set over Ignorance, Poverty, and Sickness, to deal with them as we wished. This was afterward ratified in a little chapel, to which we were led in procession, and we gave thanks to God for it. Then I hung up my Golden Fleece and my hat in God's honor, and left them there as an everlasting memorial; and since each had to write his name, I wrote thus:

Summa scientia nihil scire.
Fr. CHRISTIANUS ROSENKREUZ,
Eques aurei Lapidis:
Anno 1459.

[The height of knowledge is to know nothing. Brother Christian Rosenkreuz, Knight of the Golden Stone. In the year 1459.]

THE CHEMICAL WEDDING OF CHRISTIAN ROSENKREUZ

Others wrote otherwise, each as he saw fit. Then we were brought back into the hall and sat down, and were advised that we should consider quickly what we were going to wish for. The King and his party had gone into the little closet to hear our wishes themselves. Each one was called in there separately, so that I can say nothing about anyone else's wish. I had been thinking that nothing would be more laudable than to display some praiseworthy virtue for the honor of my Order, and now I could find none more honorable, or more hard-won, than Gratitude. Hence, although I could gladly have wished for something I desired more, I mastered myself and decided, whatever the danger, to release my benefactor the porter. When I was called in, I was first asked, since I had read the petition, whether I had noticed or suspected anything about the culprit. Thereupon I fearlessly began to relate all the events that had passed, and how I had fallen into them through ignorance, and offered to atone for all I had done. The King and the other lords were much surprised at this unexpected news, and told me to step out for a while. As soon as I returned, Atlas informed me how painful it was to His Majesty that I, beloved by him above all, should have come to such misfortune; but since they could not contravene their ancient traditions, nothing could prevent the porter from being freed, and myself put in his place. They hoped that another would soon be caught, so that I could go home again, but no release could be expected before the wedding feast of the King's future son.

This verdict nearly killed me, and I was immediately furious with myself and my blabbing mouth for not keeping quiet. But in the end I took heart, and since it seemed unavoidable I related how this porter had given me a token and recommended me to the second porter, by whose help I resisted the scales and partook of all the honor and joy I had received. Since it was only right to be grateful to one's benefactor, and as it could not be otherwise, I accepted my sentence, and was happy to accept some inconvenience that would help him in his situation. But if something could

THE CHEMICAL WEDDING OF CHRISTIAN ROSENKREUZ

still be done with my wish, I wished myself back home; thus he would be freed by me, and I by my wish.

They answered that wishes did not stretch as far as that, or else I could have simply wished him free. His Majesty was pleased that I had behaved so well, but was afraid that I did not yet realize what a sad condition my inquisitiveness had plunged me into. Now the good man was set at liberty, and I had to take my leave with a heavy heart.

After me, the others were summoned in, and all came out happy, which was all the more painful to me since I imagined that I would have to spend the rest of my life beneath the gate. I wracked my brains over what I should do and how I should spend the time. At length I concluded that I was already old, and had only a few more years to live; this misery and melancholy would soon do away with me, and then I would be done with gatekeeping. I could even bring myself into the grave by means of a peaceful sleep. I had many such thoughts. At times I was vexed that I had seen such beautiful things, and must be deprived of them. At other times I was happy that before my end I had been admitted to every joy and not sent away shamefully. This blow was the last, but also the best, that I suffered. As I meditated thus, the others made ready, and after they had bade the King and Queen good night, each was conducted to his lodging. But no one showed me the way, and I, poor fellow, had to continue in my chagrin; also, to be in no doubt of my future function, I had to put on the ring that the other had worn before me. At last the King advised me that since this was now the last time I would see him in this condition, I should conduct myself according to my position, and not against the rules of the Order. Thereupon he took me in his arms and kissed me. From all of this I understood that tomorrow I must sit by my gate. After they had all talked to me in friendship a little longer and given me their hands, they wished me God's protection, and I was led by the two old men (the gentleman of the Tower and Atlas) into a splendid bedroom where three beds stood, and each lay in one of them. There we spent almost two . . .

[About two pages in quarto are missing here, in which the Author, thinking that he must be a gatekeeper in the morning, returns home.]

THE END OF THE CHEMICAL WEDDING

About the Translators

JOSCELYN GODWIN was Professor of Music at Colgate University from 1971 to 2016. He has written and edited books on a wide range of musical and esoteric topics, and translated many more, including the *Hypnerotomachia Poliphili* of 1499, which strongly influenced the *Chemical Wedding*.

CHRISTOPHER MCINTOSH is a writer and historian specializing in the esoteric traditions of the West. He was for several years on the faculty of the Centre for the Study of Esotericism at Exeter University. He lives in Bremen, Germany.

DONATE PAHNKE MCINTOSH is a scholar of religion and, as a lecturer at the University of Bremen, specialized in Gender Studies, Esotericism, and Ritual. She runs the Selene Institute for Ritual in Bremen.

To Our Readers

Weiser Books, an imprint of Red Wheel/Weiser, publishes books across the entire spectrum of occult, esoteric, speculative, and New Age subjects. Our mission is to publish quality books that will make a difference in people's lives without advocating any one particular path or field of study. We value the integrity, originality, and depth of knowledge of our authors.

Our readers are our most important resource, and we appreciate your input, suggestions, and ideas about what you would like to see published.

Visit our website at *www.redwheelweiser.com* to learn about our upcoming books and free downloads, and be sure to go to *www.redwheelweiser.com/newsletter* to sign up for newsletters and exclusive offers.

You can also contact us at *info@rwwbooks.com* or at

Red Wheel/Weiser, LLC
65 Parker Street, Suite 7
Newburyport, MA 01950